MW01105459

A Guide for Queendom Living

Dr. Stephanie Burrage

Cover design by Malcolm McCrae

LifeRich Publishing books may be ordered through booksellers or by contacting:

LifeRich Publishing
1663 Liberty Drive
Bloomington, IN 47403
www.liferichpublishing.com
1 (888) 238-8637

ISBN: 978-1-4897-1033-8 (sc)
ISBN: 978-1-4897-1034-5 (hc)
ISBN: 978-1-4897-1032-1 (e)

Library of Congress Control Number: 2016917863

Print information available on the last page.

LifeRich Publishing rev. date: 12/6/2016

Contents

Dedication vii
Acknowledgement............ ix
Introduction............ xi

Jewel 1: Rare............ 1
Jewel 2: Trustworthy 8
Jewel 3: Constant In Her Love 14
Jewel 4: Industrious and Thrifty 21
Jewel 5: Self-Starting and Enterprising............ 27
Jewel 6: Willing To Work Hard and Long Hours............ 33
Jewel 7: Compassionate 41
Jewel 8: An Entrepreneurial Spirit And Future Planning..... 47
Jewel 9: Married To A Leader 53
Jewel 10: Not Swayed By Circumstance 62
Jewel 11: Wise 71
Jewel 12: Kindness............ 78
Jewel 13: Duty-Conscious............ 86
Jewel 14: Not Satisfied With Mediocrity............ 91
Jewel 15: A Woman Of God Who Is Worthy To Be Praised...... 99

Reference Page............ 103

Dedication

I dedicate this book to my husband, Patrick L. Burrage. As a husband, you have covered me spiritually, emotionally and prayerfully. No matter what I have wanted to do you have always provided a way to make it happen. You sacrifice so much of yourself so that I can have the things I need for my countless projects and dreams. You have been my soul mate and friend and I am always honored to be called Mrs. Patrick Burrage. Each night as I pray, I thank God for bringing us together and teaching us 1 Peter 4:8, ***"Most of all, love each other as if your life depended on it. Love makes up for practically anything."***

Also, to my beautiful children, Myles, Octavia, and Patrick, II. I hope I have instilled in you the same values of strength and perseverance that were given to me. I am so proud of the young adults you have become and I enjoy watching you navigate life as you learn more about yourself and walk in the path God has for you. You are the reason my life is complete.

Acknowledgement

To my mother, Esperanza Marie Hawkins, you instilled in me the value of overcoming all obstacles no matter what the circumstances. You have taught all of your children to be survivors and to graciously give to those who are in need. Most importantly you have taught us to always respect, honor and take care of family.

To my father, Alfred Hawkins, you instilled a very strong work ethic and provided me with the true definition of what a father and man should be to a daughter. Every female child should be fortunate enough to have a father like you.

To my focus group, friends and colleagues, Sonja Barney-Payton, Kimberly Davis, Lisa Williams, Lisa Wilmore, Victoria Hale, Alyn Moore, Pam English, Cheryl Greer, Kimberly Purifoy, Cussandra McAfee and Dr. Velicia Humes. Thank you for your comments, thoughts and honest feedback during my writing process; it was invaluable to me.

To Eric Hobson Photography, thank you for accommodating all the requests and requirements for the photo-shoot. Your professionalism was appreciated.

To my sister Mogda, thank you for challenging me to write a book at one of your first book signings and for providing insight on the publishing side of being an author.

To my pastor, Dr. Virgil Humes who teaches his flock to serve God at all times and in all places with love, compassion and humor. Thank you for your leadership, covering, teaching, mentorship and continued walk of faith.

To my brother, Michael Hawkins, your words of encouragement have always been greatly valued and appreciated.

To my grandmother, Marie Norman, whose life was a story of survival which moved me to explore the relationships of women and how they overcome, and in many cases thrive despite the obstacles they face.

To Octavia Hawkins (grandmother), S. Mae Lucas, Frieda Brown and Rosemary May, you provided me with the example of true strength, character, determination, perseverance and how to apply these skills to the many facets of my life. You embody the spirit of Harriet Tubman to inspire people beyond ordinary capabilities. I would not be the woman I am today were it not for your example.

I give all honor and praise to the Almighty for He is the author and creator of this book. Thank you for allowing me to be a vessel for your message.

Introduction

A Princess in Training for Queendom Living

"All Hail the Queen" please prepare yourself, she is about to enter the room. Hello, I am talking to you! You are the queen! If you don't know you are a queen then this book will teach you about "Queendom Living" and if you already know how to be a queen then you will receive "jewels" to help you continuously grow in your queendom. To truly understand the role of a queen in her "Queendom," we must first review the definition of queen and dominion. Merriam-Webster defines a queen as, *"a woman who rules a country or kingdom, a woman or girl who is highly respected or well-known within the field and the most powerful piece in the game of chess". Simply put, a queen is extremely powerful and well-respected. The definition of dominion is, "a territory under the control of a ruler".* An example of this could be a pastor who has dominion over his/her congregation and is responsible for the care and spiritual needs of the members.

So when we combine the words queen and dominion together, we get "Queendom" which is defined in Merriam-Webster as *"the state or territory ruled by a queen and/or the position of a queen".* In other words, she is "The most powerful and respected woman in the land with full control of her territory".

Are you operating or living under this definition of Queendom? What if every time you entered a room everyone stopped what they were doing to honor your presence? Do your children stop what they are doing to say "Good morning mom, how is your day?" Does your husband revere your name? Do random people stop and acknowledge your presence when you walk down the street? If every time you entered a room and everyone stopped what they were doing to acknowledge you then you probably would not get much done in a day, but the theory behind this concept is about knowing, living and walking in your worth. Every woman has a path to "Queendom Living" and each individual route will look completely different.

As we journey through life we make many decisions around which road to take and in what direction to travel. Some roads are less traveled and very difficult, but others are smoothly paved and easy to maneuver. As in most travel situations, people will offer directions as to the best path to follow based upon their experience. Their advice could be based upon the fact they have traveled in the same direction you are going or have never traveled your planned route, but have heard stories about the road and will try to steer you in a different direction. Friends and family will act as our own personal GPS to assist us in our journey, advising us step-by-step where to turn and what streets to avoid. In the end, as with any GPS the best directions may have to be adjusted based on unforeseen circumstances such as road construction, treacherous weather and new and improved travel conditions. When this type of change occurs we are in uncharted territory and must maneuver, the best way we can, in a new direction. The paths we take and the experiences we gain from our journey is what makes us the women we have become today. It becomes the road we travel to Queendom.

My introduction to Queendom Living started with my mother, Esperanza and my father, Alfred.

Esperanza Marie

As the story goes, my maternal grandmother married her first husband and they had children together, but at some point divorced or separated. In the 1900's if there was a separation or divorce, the mother would typically keep the children and raise them alone until she remarried. This was the case with my grandmother, who raised her children and her daughter's son after her daughter died from tuberculosis. Any woman who raises children as a single parent will tell you it is not an easy job because you have all the responsibilities related to the care of the children and the maintenance of the home or apartment. When you are a single mother taking care of all the bills and you are the everyday influencer of life, your title is CEO of your family and you don't have to practice being in charge because you are in charge, you are the leader of your family organization. When something breaks down in the house, you have to figure out a way to fix the roof, mow the grass, change the light bulbs, repair the toilets, replace tiles and manage any other maintenance repairs. So as my mother was raised in this environment, she too learned in her early childhood that the cavalry or a man would not show up to save the day and if a man did show up he may not have honorable intentions. The lesson that many women learn through experience or observation is not to depend on any one or a man to get things done because in order to survive you must, as the Nike slogan states, "Just Do It". Based on my mother's experiences in her home she developed a belief system to ensure her daughters would be college educated so as not to have to depend on anyone for assistance. In my mother's generation, everyone did not go to college. Many women stayed home to care for the family or they held jobs that did not require a degree which made women dependent on the husband or, if single, made the women unable to support her family financially based on her meager income.

So from the beginning of time, my mother, Esperanza, made sure my sister and I understood we had to go to college to be able to "financially take good care of ourselves". In her next breath my mother would say "if a man doesn't do what he is supposed to do then you will always be able to take care of yourself and not be dependent on any man because every man is not like your father and will not take care of you like him". Next would come the lessons around men and her nuggets to us, "If you allow a man to use you one time, he will do it over and over again, then talk about how stupid you are to his friends", "Always be ok to walk away from any man or person who does not honor who you are in life", "A man will always see you as a fool if you allow him to walk over you and you just take it, his view of you will never change", "Never let a man put his hands on you ever! If he hits you once he will hit you again, so get out of that situation as fast as you can and then worry about me coming for you for allowing that nonsense!", "Don't ever be the other woman because a man will only see you as such and you will compromise yourself in the process" and my personal favorite "I didn't raise you to be stupid, so have plan A, B, C and D and think your way out of all situations, don't embarrass me by not thinking".

Alfred

My father was born in Chicago, but was raised in a small town in southwest Michigan on a 100-acre farm from the age of seven. His parents lived in Chicago during the week and would come to the farm on the weekend to get produce to take back and sell in Chicago. His older brother and his wife were the custodial parents when my grandparents were not at home, but this meant my father had to be extremely responsible at a young age and had to manage himself. As he grew up, he worked the farm and was very active in school. My father made sure all school documents were turned in on time and signed in the place of his parents due to their frequent absence.

My father met and started dating my mother when they were fourteen and fifteen respectively, as they were both from neighboring towns and each had family members who had married. My father attended a Midwestern university and after the first year returned home to get my mother. They married in July and moved into married housing for the fall. My father shared with my mother that he would finish college and then she would complete her bachelor's degree. Once she finished with her bachelor's degree then he would get a master's degree and she would follow him with a master's degree. Once she finished her master's degree, he followed with his educational specialist degree and my mother said she was fine not going back to school, her master's was enough. His plan was to work and pay cash for their college degrees, which is what he did. He believed in always taking care of his family financially and worked extra jobs to make ends meet and did not live beyond his means. He was always calm under pressure and there was not any problem that did not have a solution; if you just have faith it will all work out in the end. When we were older and my mother would want certain things like jewelry and perfume, my father would say, "Your mother can get what she wants because when you kids were younger she sacrificed for the family and would get clothes from Goodwill to make my budget work...this is her time and she can have whatever she wants". My father was about following and executing a plan of action. If he said he was going to do something, he did it; he has always been a man of his word.

The Princess Training Years

I was raised by both parents, a mother who was raised independently and a father who was the best father in the world and who took care of everything for my siblings and me. My dad is the epitome of a great father; he attended all my activities, made sure all of our needs were met, was there for counsel, was not judgmental and he never complained. He was very active in the church and made sure we attended service every Sunday. In fact, if I call my dad today, the first words from his mouth are, "How is my darling daughter?" So in my world I always listened to my mother's stories and even followed her company line about questioning all men, however, I lived a different life than my mother because I trusted my father completely....I was treated by my father as a princess and was being groomed for queendom. I could be and am independent by choice which is a different perspective. So even though I heard and respected the stories from my mother, my aunts and the elder women who helped raise me and I could relate intellectually, I did not live their experience. I actually looked forward to my father's opinions and valued his perspective because it always helped me to look at all sides of a problem which ultimately helped me make better decisions.

I spent quite a bit of time with my father when I was younger because my mother and her good friend, Rosemary, were working towards their master's degrees. I was in high school and while they were in classes at night, my father was the point parent. I spent so much time with him that he was able to pour his knowledge and views into me which has always helped me understand the different perspective and views of men. I didn't know it at the time but my dad was teaching me how to communicate with my future king. This type of communication with my father helped me communicate with my husband. I am not going to say my husband and I are perfect in our communication style, but I listen to hear his voice, seek his counsel in decisions and respect his opinions.

This type of relationship with my dad helped me navigate the language of men as I started dating. It was always easy for me to discern early on if a relationship was going to progress beyond taking me out to dinner and a movie. I could tell in the first date if the guy was worth me continuing to a second date based on his language, conversational style and how he treated and interacted with me. If the guy did not have an easy going relationship style and did not put me first, then he didn't last long. When going on a date, if a young man didn't come to the door to pick me up, open the door when we approached the car, helped me out of the car, assist me with my coat and make sure I was ok before we sat down at the restaurant or movie, then I knew this man had not been raised to care for me the way I expected. Based on my relationship with my dad, I didn't operate from a place of lack with men; I operated from a place of abundance which equated to having high expectations of the men I allowed in my space. If a young man was unable to care for me at the same level my dad took care of me then I had no problem stating this was not going to work and we did not have to continue dating. I had already seen the blueprint of excellence in my dad, so my spirit is most comfortable with someone who cares for me and will put my needs before his own.

Both of my parents were preparing me for Queendom Living, prepping me to be the most powerful and respected woman in the land with full control of her territory. My job is not to take over the Kingdom but to be respected, loved, revered, listened to and honored in my territory, if there is a king present or not! As I shared earlier, we all make our way to Queendom Living and the road I took may look totally different than your path.

The father I have may look totally different from the father you have however, we all strive to be the best queen we can be in the Queendom.

Queendom Living is about the journey and learning how powerful and special we are in our own territory. Proverbs 31:30 states, ***"Charm can mislead and beauty soon fades. The woman to be admired and praised is the woman who lives in the Fear of God".***

It is our relationship or oneness with God which allows us to transfer our kindness, forgiveness, compassion, trust, understanding, mercy, grace and love to our husbands, children, family and neighbors. We learn through our relationship with God to transfer these jewels to the people in our Queendom. This is not an easy job and it is not for the faint of heart but it is the most rewarding job and the place where we can apply and model love and forgiveness on a day to day basis.

As I studied Proverbs 31, I realized this chapter defined the qualities of a virtuous woman. Proverbs 31 provides the job description for how to be the best wife, mother, sister, neighbor and friend. I saw these qualities as "jewels" to live by. It is the inspiration for the writing of this book so that every woman can recognize and understand her role as a wife, mother, sister, neighbor and friend. As I studied each jewel I realized I had to be honest with myself. There were some jewels which I represented well and there were other jewels that I struggled with because I did not exhibit the qualities of those jewels. Studying the jewels guided my transformation on the inside, which manifested change on the outside. Living the jewels is not about changing your spouse or anyone else, it is all about self-transformation!

As queens we are all on this journey and I want you to know the benefit of each jewel and understand we are all working towards representing our best selves in all situations. The intention is not to focus on each jewel and check it off your list of accomplishments but to be accountable and strive to exhibit what each jewel embodies through grace, strength and prayer. I want you to know the benefit of living each jewel builds the foundation of a successful, joyous, happy and fulfilling life and or marriage. I pray you find the "jewels" in this book will give you the tools to live happily ever after with your King and provide you with love, joy and peace as you reign in your Queendom. Enjoy!

Jewel: Rare

Proverbs 31:10
"A good woman is hard to find, and worth far more than diamonds."

I love to ask couples how they met, but I particularly like to ask men what they loved most about their spouse when they first started dating. Once they get past physical appearance or funny actions, the responses move to characteristics of the wife. There is always a stand-out characteristic or rare quality a man looks for in a woman based on their past or something that touches their soul. I, too, have asked my husband, Patrick, this question around what rare qualities did he see in me that stood out to him when we first met? Once Patrick realized it was not a trick question and I really wanted an authentic answer, I was surprised by his answer and how my qualities were interconnected with his mother. Patrick shared there were several unique qualities he observed over 25 years ago, which he still loves today. He loves my energetic spirit and respect for individuals. These unique qualities made me stand out to him years ago and aligned with his mother's ways. Patrick describes his mother as very helpful, loving everyone and always doing things as a family. One of his favorite activities with his mom was cooking together weekly. My husband is the "official" cook in our family, so I have never been required to take on this task because it is something that he loves to do; cooking relaxes him and his food is presented like you are in a fine restaurant and tastes simply amazing. I know when my husband cooks, he is able to bring his mother's love and care for people through her recipes to our table. Being a chef is not on my bucket list and in the hierarchical cooking structure in our home I am last on the list, even behind the children. Patrick made sure all of our children can cook, especially the boys, because as his mother told him "you may fall in love with a woman who does not cook and someone has to feed the family"; his mother also had wisdom. Now, I may not cook but I am the official assistant and my duties range from cutting vegetables, cleaning the pots and getting any ingredient he is missing while he cooks. I tell stories and jokes to keep him company while he is in the kitchen. The rare quality Patrick enjoys in me is not about the work I do in the kitchen, but how I make him feel appreciating his gift of cooking for our family. When I am with him while he cooks, he swears I am his inspiration for our meals. I like to define myself as his cooking muse! So cooking in our family is more than just nourishment to our bodies, it is a family activity everyone can and does participate in by prepping, cooking, eating and talking over each meal.

Rare Qualities

What makes a woman rare? Every woman has the same physical features such as a nose, eyes and lips but it is our individual differences which make us unique. Our eye colors can range from brown, blue and aqua green, while our noses can range from small to grand. Rare and Unique qualities are described as having a higher value compared to something similar in nature. An example would be the Hope Diamond, an extremely rare jewel, housed at the Smithsonian. The Hope Diamond is similar to other diamonds, however its size of 45.52 carats makes it one of the largest diamonds in the world and "it's much admired blue color is due to trace amounts of boron atoms (1)". The Hope Diamond is so rare it is one of the most visited museum objects in the world.

Why do people search for rare things? I believe most people want to say they have the "one special thing" in the world. The work required to find something rare and unique is enormous but people will spend days, months, years, even decades to find something rare.

So maybe the question is not what makes a woman rare but what is a rare woman? How do you identify the concept of rare? Do you see yourself as precious? Someone to be treasured? *Genesis 2: 22-23 states, "Then the Lord God made a woman from the rib he had taken out of man, and he brought her to the man." The man said, "This is now bone of my bones and flesh of my flesh; she shall be called 'woman' for she was taken out of man."*

Woman were created rare, taken from the rib of man and created by God in His likeness. Our assignment is to be a helpmate to man but to also carry and bear life. We have been given the unique gift to cultivate another human being in our body. The process of carrying children does not happen quickly but takes up to nine months, 40 weeks or 252 days. Every thought we have, food we eat, songs we sing, music we listen to and feelings we have connects with the precious life form we carry in our wombs. Some women even have the uncommon experience to carry multiple children at one time. Our work does not end when we give birth, but it is just the beginning of a lifetime of caring for our young (even when they are grown). The gift of motherhood can come in many forms whether it is carrying a child in the womb, surrogacy, adoption or foster care. The bond or connection between a mother and child is usually only broken through death. Early in my teaching career, there was a first grade student who, for all practical purposes was taking care of his younger brother and sister. This student would come to school and save part of his food at breakfast and lunch and take it home to his siblings. Child protection services was called and we found out the mother was leaving the first grader in their apartment at night to take care of his younger brother and sister. When a social worker came to pick up the student from school and take him to a foster home this mild mannered child screamed and fought not to get in the car. He yelled, cried and beat the car window to get to his mother. I remember watching him lose it in the back seat of the social workers car trying to get to his mother. It made me think that no matter how bad it gets we still want a connection, bad or good, to our mother.

Like precious jewels it takes time to cultivate our "woman-ness". The rarest and most precious jewels can take millions of years to form in nature. Like rare and precious jewels God is taking the time to grow and cultivate you into the woman He has called you to be. Are you living in your purpose? Are you using your talents and gifts for His purpose? Do you embody the characteristics of an excellent woman?

You will know you are walking in your purpose and living a life of excellence when you put the Lord above all things and your family praises your name. You will exhibit the jewels of strength, wisdom, caring, compassion, forgiveness and love in all your conversations. Several characteristics make up this rare woman but it is her relationship with God and her reverence to Him which make her more precious than rubies. I recommend you place Proverbs 31:30, "Charm can mislead and beauty soon fades. The woman to be admired and praised is the woman who lives in Fear-of- God" on your bathroom mirror so that every morning when you arise you will start your day by putting the word of God in your heart to realize your role and full potential through Him.

Proverbs 31:30, "Charm can mislead and beauty fades. The woman to be praised is the woman who lives in Fear of God".

PERSONAL REFLECTION

1. What makes a woman as valuable as a rare jewel? Do you know any women who fit your description of such a jewel?

2. What "rare" qualities do you possess?

3. What areas in your life would you need to adjust to acquire a few more "rare" qualities than you currently possess?

HELPFUL STUDY

- ❖ Ruth 3:11, "Now, my daughter, do not fear. I will do for you whatever you ask, for all my people in the city know that you are a woman of excellence."

- ❖ Proverbs 8:11, "For wisdom is better than jewels; And all desirable things cannot compare with her."

- ❖ Proverbs 14:1, "The wise woman builds her house, but the foolish tears it down with her own hands."

- Proverbs 18:22, "He who finds a wife finds a good thing and obtains favor from the LORD."

- Proverbs 19:14, "House and wealth are an inheritance from fathers, but a prudent wife is from the LORD."

Odd Tales from the Smithsonian (Smithsonian Institution Press, 1986), written by Peggy Thomson and Edwards Park.

Jewel: Trustworthy

Proverbs 31:11
"Her husband trusts her without reserve,
and never has reason to regret it."

Trustworthiness is so important because it is the anchor or foundation of a relationship. When you trust someone, you know how he or she will respond in good times and in a crisis. That person will not change who he or she is because of the situation. When Dominique met Bill, her husband of 50 years, she tells the story of how Bill gave her his paycheck totaling $800 for Dominique to "hold". Dominique rolled up the money, put it in a sock and placed the sock in her drawer until Bill returned later for the money. When Bill came back two weeks later and asked for the money, Dominique pulled it from the sock and gave it to him. Dominique was honored that Bill trusted her to hold that much money for him and Bill trusted Dominique not to spend his hard earned money and to keep it safe until he needed the cash.

When you have someone's trust, you also have their ear and they will seek your voice for counsel. You become a confidante in the relationship, and the expectation is that you will honor the information shared by not repeating or using it against the person. When mistrust presents itself in a relationship and the bond is broken, then the foundation the trust was built on must be rebuilt for secure footing. Building trust takes time and patience. Your words must match your actions at all times.

Sampson and Delilah

Sampson was one of the last judges of his era and served in this role for 20 years. He was also a Nazirite which means he could not drink wine, eat grapes or raisins, could not cut his hair or be around any dead body for this was considered unclean.

Living the Nazirite lifestyle showed his commitment to God and served as an example to the people of Israel. Sampson had killed a lion and carried away the huge gate of Gaza so he was known for his physical strength. Using this great prowess, Sampson killed thousands of the Philistine people who were enemies of the Israelite people. Sampson met and fell in love with a woman named Delilah. When the Philistine leaders learned of his feelings for Delilah, they offered her money to find the source of his strength so they could bind and kill him. Delilah tried day and night to seduce Sampson to tell her the truth of his strength. On three occasions, Sampson gave Delilah a different story to hide his strength and each time her plan was unsuccessful. It was the fourth time when Delilah used her seductive words to open his heart that he told her everything, Judges 16:17, *"No razor has ever been used on my head, because I have been a Nazirite dedicated to God from my mother's womb. If my head were shaved, my strength would leave me, and I would become as weak as any other man."* When Delilah heard his heart she had Sampson go to sleep, called the Philistine leaders and she and one of the leaders shaved his hair making him weak so the Philistine leaders could capture him.

As we reflect on this story, we have to ask ourselves why was Sampson so naïve and trusting of Delilah? Sampson wanted Delilah to love him at any cost and because of his weakness he was blinded to her dishonest nature. Sampson was aware of Delilah's three unsuccessful attempts to find his weakness. These failed attempts should have opened his eyes to her lack of trustworthiness. On Delilah's fourth attempt to find his weakness, Sampson fell into sin, as we all fall into sin and like us, Sampson could not see the truth in front of him.

Are You Trustworthy?

Any time you paint a picture of yourself that does not represent who you truly are, it can eventually open the door to suspicion, distrust or utter disappointment. Your intent is to always be a woman of your word, while understanding we all fall short of the kingdom of God (Romans 3:23). We have all sinned but because God sent his only son to die on the cross for us, his blood was the price for our sin. As believers we all fall short but this does not mean we must live in our mistakes forever. Thankfully our debt was paid through the blood of Jesus Christ and we didn't have to do anything to receive it! If you have done something to misrepresent the truth then apologize and work on building the foundation of your relationship. If your trust in someone has been shattered then ask God to assist you with forgiveness. Learn how to show grace and mercy when someone falls short of your expectations because when the table turns you will want the same grace and mercy for yourself.

Examples of how mistrust can hinder the foundation of a relationship.

- ✓ As a couple, you have agreed to save money but several new pairs of shoes and new clothes are hidden in the house.

- ✓ You agree to pay certain bills as a plan of action and you don't pay the bills or share the change in plans.

- ✓ Taking money from the saving or checking account without discussion.

- ✓ Cheating or having an affair with another person.

- ✓ Saying you are free from STD's but you are not.
- ✓ Saying you are with friends but are actually somewhere else (casino, movie, etc.).
- ✓ Telling your spouse or significant other you want children but never intend to have children.
- ✓ Faking pregnancy.
- ✓ Talking negatively about your spouse or significant other and his/her family.
- ✓ Not supportive of your spouses' dreams.
- ✓ Not sharing your complete financial picture.
- ✓ Saying one thing and doing another.

PERSONAL REFLECTION

1. Has someone every broken your trust? What was the circumstance and how did it affect your relationship?
2. Have you ever misrepresented the truth? What was the occasion? What was the outcome?
3. What makes you a trustworthy person?

When you have someone's trust, you also have their ear and they will seek your voice for counsel.

HELPFUL STUDY

- Proverbs 12:4, "An excellent wife is the crown of her husband, but she who shames him is like rottenness in his bones."

- 1 Peter 3:1-4, "The same goes for you wives: Be good wives to your husbands, responsive to their needs. There are husbands who, indifferent as they are to any words about God, will be captivated by your holy beauty. What matters is not your outer appearance – the style of your hair, the jewelry you wear, the cut of your clothes – but your inner disposition."

Jewel: Constant In Her Love

Proverbs 31:12
"Never spiteful, she treats him generously all her life long."

Early in their marriage, a young couple had an issue with parking tickets. The husband had several unpaid parking tickets and the wife continually asked the husband to pay them. The young couple was out with their two young children driving to a mall when the police pulls the young couple over. The police officer told the husband that he was driving 5 miles over the speed limit and asked for his driver's license, proof of registration and insurance. The officer went back to his patrol car to run the license plate and returned to the vehicle. He shared with the husband there was a warrant for his arrest for unpaid parking tickets so he would have to take him to jail. He asked the husband to exit the vehicle, placed him in hand cuffs and put him in the back of the police patrol car. When the father left the vehicle his children were terrified and they asked their mother, "What is going to happen to daddy; will the police shoot him?" The young mother calmed the children and used her current situation as a lesson; she talked to them about the importance of driving the speed limit because when you drive too fast, the police will give you a ticket to slow you down and not hurt other drivers. She assured the children their father would be ok and went to the police station to get her husband out of jail.

When the young mother arrived at the police station she calmly talked to a police officer about the process to pay for the unpaid parking tickets and the money required to pay the bail for her husband. The police officer shared with the wife that her husband's behavior was less than favorable while in their care. The young wife calmly and politely said this was not her husband's normal behavior and this situation was unsettling as her husband was arrested in front of their young children. She agreed to pay all fines to get him out of jail immediately. She asked the police officer if she could see her husband momentarily to let him know that she is in the process of getting him out of jail, knowing this information might settle him down. The police officer honored her request and the young wife told her husband what she was doing to get him out of jail. When the husband was released from jail and got back in the car, the wife asked if he was ok and did he want to go home or continue to the mall? She did not tell the husband, "I told you to pay the tickets" but checked on him again to see if he was alright.

As a woman, it is our responsibility to be a shield for our family, as the young wife learned she had to stand and represent her husband when his behavior was less than favorable. The young wife had to speak on her husband's behalf in his time of need to make things endurable. Being constant in her love is not an easy jewel because one must represent this quality in and out of season; during good and bad times. Our role is not to constantly berate our husband(s) for past mistakes but to live in our role of help mate. There is not a person who wants to hear their mistakes brought up to them over and over again for a 20, 30, 40 or 50 year period of time. Being constant in her love is a hard jewel because your first thoughts would be to tell your spouse "I told you to pay the tickets" or to rant and rave about all the other things he has not done in the past decade. Does this sound familiar? This type of behavior does not represent "Queendom Living" or the jewel constant in her love. The young wife's calm demeanor shielded her husband and their children. She was able to teach several lessons to her children about the consequences of not following the rules, staying calm in stressful situations, forgiveness and respect. In all relationships there is a give and take, it is never equal. There are times when one person in the relationship will give 99 percent while the other person only has 1 percent to give.

Abigail's Story

The story of Abigail found in 1 Samuel 25: 18-31 is an example of a woman who was constant in her love to a husband who was undeserving of her love. Abigail's husband, Nabal, was a very rich man with many possessions. He was also mean, nasty and lived up to the meaning of his name as "foolish". One day King David sent his men in peace to Nabal requesting assistance with sheep shearing. King David was expecting reciprocal support as King David did not take advantage of Nabal's men when they were in his presence previously. As King David's men shared his request and the previous support, Nabal insulted King David and did not acknowledge the past support provided by King David. The offense to King David was so severe and egregious, that King David put a plan in motion to kill Nabal and destroy everything he owned.

Nabal's servant informed Abigail of King David's plan and she flew into action, 1 Samuel 25:18-19 states, *"She took two hundred loaves of bread, two skins of wine, five sheep dressed and ready for cooking, a bushel of roasted grain, a hundred raisin cakes, and two hundred fig cakes, and she had it all loaded on donkeys. Then she said to her young servant, "Go ahead and pave the way for me. I'm right behind you."* But she said nothing to her husband, Nabal. When Abigail saw King David she bowed down before him in honor and told King David she would accept all the blame for her husband and asked King David to listen to her. Abigail shared with King David that her husband was a horribly wicked man and asked that he not pay him any attention because Nabal was a fool as is the meaning of his name. Abigail presented the gifts of food and wine and asked for forgiveness if she had offended King David in any way. Abigail also shared with King David his greatness in the eyes of God and how it would be unnecessary for such a powerful man to waste his time killing Nabal, a man of insignificance, by destroying all of his possessions. King David accepted Abigail's gifts and sent her home in peace. When Abigail arrived home, Nabal had a feast in his home that was fit for a king with wine and merriment. Nabal was intoxicated so Abigail waited until the morning to share with him everything that had happened. When Nabal heard the story he had a stroke and died 10 days later.

When Nabal offended King David, Abigail could have taken the stance that her husband was a fool and he deserved to be punished for his actions and let everyone suffer the consequences because of his nastiness and stupidity. Abigail put the needs of her husband, even though Nabal had created this situation, before her own to protect her husband, herself and his servants. She did not lie about his behavior or make excuses, but she intervened in the situation and spoke humbly on Nabal's behalf. Abigail exhibited self-control and kept a clear head through her ordeal. She did not call her friends and bad mouth her husband, and she did not wallow in pity. Instead she developed a plan of action. Abigail's actions represent the characteristics of a woman being constant in her love because she did not waiver.

What does being "Constant in Her Love" look like?

A shield of protection is:

- Looking beyond someone's faults
- Not pointing out flaws
- Never saying "I told you so"
- Being positive and sweet with your language (The tongue is the most powerful muscle)
- Prayer

The Apostle Paul instructed all Christians to pray for one another, Ephesians 6:18. It is a privilege and our responsibility to pray for our husbands. Intense prayer for your spouse is good for him, for you and the spiritual health and well-being of your home. The enemy desires to destroy your husband, especially his character and his leadership in your relationship. Trust God through prayer as you surrender your husband and marriage to the Almighty's loving care. Remember, God takes care of you in the same way so it is our job to model to others how he treats us every day.

PERSONAL REFLECTION

1. How often do we see the characteristic of being constant in love in action? We talk about a parent's love for their children being unconditional and unwavering but what about our spouses?

2. What happens when a spouse has unfavorable characteristics? What actions can you take to show unconditional love for your spouse?

3. Did you pray about your situation and give it over to God for direction?

4. Seek patience and a clear head.

5. Seek self-control – This means be very thoughtful with who you share your current situation or problems and avoid "paying someone back" for your hurt.

6. Do all things through love because love unites. Are you a loving person? Whatever your answer, work towards a loving spirit. Love is an action.

HELPFUL STUDY

- Luke 6:35-36, "I tell you, love your enemies. Help and give without expecting a return. You'll never—I promise---regret it. Live out this God-created identity the way our Father lives toward us, generously and graciously, even when were at our worst. Our Father is kind; you be kind."

- 1 John 4:8, "Who ever does not love does not know God, because God is love."

- 1 Corinthians 13:4-8, "Love never gives up, love cares more for others than self, love doesn't want what it doesn't have, love doesn't strut, doesn't have a swelled head, doesn't force itself on others, isn't always "me first", doesn't fly off the handle, doesn't keep score or the sins of others, doesn't revel when others grovel, takes pleasure in the flowering of truth, puts up with anything, trusts God always, always looks for the best, never looks back, but keeps going to the end."

- 1 Peter 4:8, "Most of all, love each other as if your life depended on it. Love makes up for practically anything."

Jewel: Industrious and Thrifty

Proverbs 31:13-14

"She shops around for the best yarns and cottons, and enjoys knitting and sewing. She's like a trading ship that sails away to faraway places and brings back exotic surprises."

Marlene and Blake had been together for 20 years and had two teenage children. Blake was a real estate agent when the housing market crashed and he lost his job. Blake had been without work for five months when he was offered a job in another state six hours from home. Blake did not want to work out of state and away from his family but they were in the hole financially. The mortgage had not been paid for the last three months and Blake could not bring himself to tell Marlene they were moving into month four. Blake accepted the job and worked out of state during the week and came home on the weekends. During the time Blake was not working, Marlene was determined the children and the family would not feel the weight of the family's financial burden so she worked two extra jobs to make ends meet for her family.

In high school Marlene, learned to sew in Home Economics class and sewed for enjoyment, but now she had to sew for necessity because they did not have money for the store-bought designer clothing her daughter was used to wearing every year to school. Marlene took her daughter to the fabric store to find fabric, colors and styles to her daughter's liking for the first two dresses and shirts. She asked her daughter to help her because she was going to "try her hand at sewing again" and needed her daughter to act as a model for her and help her practice. Whenever possible Marlene would still go to the stores to look for clothing deals but only shopped clearance or 70 to 80 percent mark downs at a store. Marlene understood her family's financial situation because the bill collectors called the house when Blake was not home and aggressively requested payment options for the past due bills. Each time they called she referenced them back to Blake because he handled the bills. Marlene was determined to still live their normal way of life but with adjustments. Instead of family vacations in exotic places the family camped in tents at different camp sites or had staycations and visited free museums and discounted parks in the area. Instead of eating at fast food restaurants whenever it suited them, Marlene cooked breakfast every morning and dinner every night to save on food costs. Blake and Marlene lived this way for several years until they were able to climb out of debt.

An Industrious Woman

Who is an industrious woman and what does she look like? An industrious woman leads by example in her walk with God which makes her extremely responsible because she puts the needs of others before her own. An industrious woman is hard working, conscientious and diligent. We typically define her as the "Woman" of the house and you see her in the Queendom always taking care of her business and making it happen for her family. The position of woman of the house is an honor and an extensive job. Remember the queen is the most powerful position in the queendom because she has the ear and knowledge of all her family members in her territory. The work of the industrious woman is to exemplify God in all things while honoring all God has given her; in abundance and deficit. She knows everything going on in her home because she has a watchful eye and understands when something is off balance and addresses it immediately.

In the story, the husband handled the financial matters but that is not the case in every home. Regardless of who handles the finances, the industrious woman is thrifty and manages the financial needs of her home with a prudent and watchful eye. Family members will use words to describe her as sensible, wise, practical, far-sighted, cautious, careful and discreet. We see this woman at the grocery store with her clipped coupons trying to make the grocery money stretch or always looking on the clearance rack first for the best deals for clothing. She teaches budgeting skills and works to live within the financial means of the family. She practices tithes and offerings, savings and paying the bills in a timely manner.

Her jewels shine brightly through her actions and characteristics:

1. Loves God with all her heart and soul!

2. Has established a spiritual relationship and surrounds herself with other believers.

3. Provides meals for her family.

4. Prays daily for her family and community at large.

5. Studies the word as a family.

6. Makes sure the house is maintained.

7. Makes time for family.

8. Exemplifies love, joy, peace, patience, kindness, goodness, faithfulness, gentleness and self-control (*The Fruits of the Spirit is found in Galatians 5:22-23.)*

9. Presents herself with grace and class.

10. Mentors other women

11. Her voice is valued in the home

12. Lives in wisdom.

PERSONAL REFLECTION

1. Have you ever had to put the needs of someone else before yours for the good of a cause? Describe the situation.

2. How do you keep a pulse on what is happening in your home?

3. Who manages the finances in the home? Do you have a weekly or monthly budget? Do you practice savings? Do you tithe regularly?

HELPFUL STUDY

❖ Proverbs 6:6-8, "Look at the ant. Watch it closely; let it teach you a thing or two. Nobody has to tell it what to do. All summer it stores up food; at harvest it stockpiles provisions."

❖ 2 Thessalonians 3:10, "Don't you remember the rule we had when we lived with you? If you don't work you don't eat."

❖ Philippians 4:13, "Whatever I have, wherever I am, I can make it through anything in the One who makes me who I am."

- Proverbs 27:23-27, "Know your sheep by name; carefully attend to your flocks; (Don't take them for granted; possessions don't last forever, you know). And then, when the crops are in and the harvest is stored in the barns, you can knit sweaters from lambs' wool, and sell your goats for a profit; there will be plenty of milk and meat to last your family through the winter."

Jewel: Self-Starting and Enterprising

Proverbs 31: 15-16
"She is up before dawn, preparing breakfast for her family and organizing her day. She looks over a field and buys it, then with money she's put aside, plants a garden."

The first home I lived in was a three-bedroom home on Phillips Street in South Haven where my parents shared a bedroom, my sister and I shared a bedroom, and my brother had his own room being the only boy. My grandmother lived with us and shared the room with my brother for a period of time until she moved down the street to an apartment. When my mother decided it was time to move the family to a larger home for her growing family, she started the conversations, with my dad and a woman named Stephanie, about moving to the right neighborhood and getting the most house for their money. Stephanie was a personal friend and mentor to my mother who was considered well-to-do in social circles. My mother said Stephanie and her looked at homes all over our city and found the home my parents still live in today, 41 years later. What my mother loved about the home was that it was a ranch style house with three bedrooms, two bathrooms, a front room, full kitchen, family room, spacious yard and the potential to expand. The vision and foresight of my mother and the financial mind of my father allowed them to enlarge their home over the next 40 years with two additions to the home, an in-ground pool and the additional purchase of the property next door for more yard space. Their home has been the place for family reunions and many family gatherings as their family has grown to include husbands and wives of their children, grand-children and great-grand-children.

To make this plan work, my father had to work additional jobs and my mother had to sacrifice in areas for the benefit of the family. My father shares the story of how my mother shopped at Goodwill instead of purchasing new clothes for the family or how there were times they wanted to go out but it was not in the budget.

Lydia

While the Apostle Paul traveled on a missionary journey he received a vision of a man from Macedonia praying for Paul to, *"Come over to Macedonia, and help us" Acts 16:9.* After receiving the vision, Paul and Silas travel to Philippi, the capitol of Macedonia and searched for people to teach The Gospel. A synagogue did not exist in the area so Paul and Silas go to the riverside, a usual place of prayer. Paul and Silas sit down and begin to speak to the women who are gathered at the river for prayer. Acts16: 14-15 states, *"One woman, Lydia, was from Thyatira and a dealer in expensive textiles, known to be a God-fearing woman. As she listened with intensity to what was being said, the Master gave her a trusting heart—and she believed! After she was baptized, along with everyone in her household, she said in a surge of hospitality, "If you're confident that I'm in this with you and believe in the Master truly, come home with me and be my guest." We hesitated, but she wouldn't take no for an answer."*

The characteristics of a self-starting and enterprising woman is a woman who is resourceful and takes the initiative without needing encouragement from others. She plants seeds for the future of her family to nurture and grow over the years. Lydia is an example of a self-starting and enterprising woman. Lydia did not let the lack of a synagogue stop her and the other women from praying. As Lydia was already a believer she was unable to start a synagogue, which at the time required ten Jewish men to commence, she started a Christian community at the river and in her territory. Lydia believed in the power of pray and understood prayer changes all things and as Mathew 18: 19-20 states, *"When two of you get together on anything at all on earth and make a prayer of it, my Father in heaven goes into action. And when two or three of you are together because of me, you can be sure that I'll be there."*

As Paul delivered the word of God to Lydia, she spoke to Paul in a public setting, as this was not customary among Jews for women to speak in public. Having access and exposure to the Gospel freed Lydia from gender restrictions assigned to females at the time. Lydia's belief in God made her the first Gentile European convert to Christianity and because of her work through her prayer community she became a church founder and a leader.

What can we take away from the self-starting and enterprising jewel?

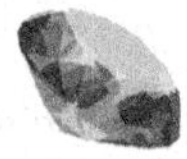

1. Don't let your fears prevent you from following your destiny. When you are living in your destiny, everyone may not always agree with or encourage you in your journey. You must learn to encourage yourself and know your path may be a model for someone else.

2. When you are blessed with a gift or resources, use them freely to benefit others. Lydia had the gift of hospitality and she may not have been able to do anything else but provide Paul and those with him a place to stay to meet their needs.

3. You don't want to lose your gifts by not using them or keeping them to yourself. Appreciate all that you are given so that when you are elevated to the next level, you will gain a better understanding of what you need to continue to grow.

4. Be patient. All things will materialize in the day and time it is supposed to occur. There may be times when you want something so badly you are willing to compromise your values for the benefit of immediate gratification. Stay focused and wait for the time when there is no question about the direction or path you need to take.

5. Open your heart, listen and serve.

PERSONAL REFLECTION

1. How do you exhibit the self-starting and enterprising qualities?

2. What personal gifts and talents do you possess? How are you utilizing your talents and gifts?

3. What traditions get in the way of your development and growth?

4. Has there been a time when you did not follow your heart? What got in the way?

5. Do you have a 5, 10, 15, 20-year plan? If not, create one to formulate your dreams into an action plan for the future.

6. What are you willing to sacrifice to increase your territory?

7. Sit down and write a short and long term plan for your personal and professional life.

HELPFUL STUDY

- Habakkuk 2:3, "The message I give you waits for the time I have appointed. It speaks about what is going to happen. And all of it will come true. It might take a while. But wait for it. You can be sure it will come. It will happen when I want it to."

- Proverbs 20:13, "Don't be too fond of sleep; you'll end up in the poorhouse. Wake up and get up; then there'll be food on the table."

- Matthew 13:44, "God's kingdom is like a treasure hidden in a field for years and then accidentally found by a trespasser. The finder is ecstatic—what a find!—and proceeds to sell everything he owns to raise money and buy that field."

- James 2:26, "The very moment you separate body and spirit, you end up with a corpse. Separate faith and works and you get the same thing: a corpse."

Jewel: Willing To Work Hard and Long Hours

Proverbs 31:17
"First thing in the morning, she dresses for work, rolls up her sleeves, eager to get started. She senses the worth of her work, is in no hurry to call it quits for the day. She's skilled in the crafts of home and hearth diligent in homemaking."

Macey was looking forward to the next year with anticipation and longing as her son Mario was starting his senior year and would participate in his senior activities such as beautillion, prom, senior night, graduation and his open house party. Macey was very detailed and had already started planning for the different activities and had a month by month schedule to follow. When she presented the schedule to her husband Rome to follow, he laughed and told her to settle down and stop over planning their son growing up. Rome did not understand that each event took preparation and detailed scheduling to make this year the best year for Mario. Macey had been extremely tired lately and thought it was connected to all the activities going on in their family life and decided she would stop by the grocery store and get a multivitamin to boost her energy. She was also hoping the small lump she felt two months ago would go away because it was starting to bother her and it was getting bigger. She did not have time to go to the doctor's office with track practice and games for Mario taking up all of her time. Macey did not have a family history of breast cancer so it was not an immediate concern but she knew she should go get it checked. Macey did not tell Rome about the lump because she did not want him to worry and she did not want to hear Rome say "I told you so" about not taking care of herself. A month later Macey was so tired and could not shake the flu like symptoms she made an appointment with her family physician. While Macey was talking to her doctor she showed her the lump that would not go away. The doctor was concerned and scheduled a mammogram for Macey the next day. Macey did not have time to go to the appointment because her son had a track meet in the afternoon but her doctor would not take no for an answer so she would just have to go to the track meet late. As Macey sat in the office waiting for the technician she used the time to adjust her monthly schedule to accommodate a new meeting with the mothers on the track team around snacks and travel for the year. The next day Macey received a call from her doctor to make an appointment that afternoon to discuss the results; she knew something was wrong. Macey's physician would not call her into the office if the results were not serious. When Macey's physician told her she had breast cancer, her world stopped moving and for a moment she thought "how am I going to schedule cancer into my life?"

The Woman with the Issue of Blood

Mark 5: 25-34 tells the story of a woman who was sick and had hemorrhaged blood for 12 years. This woman had spent her earnings on many different doctors to cure her disease, but was still sick and getting worse. As this woman was in the crowd near Jesus she came behind him and touched his clothes with the belief and faith that if she could just touch his clothing, she would be healed from her disease. Immediately the woman with the issue of blood stopped hemorrhaging and was cured of her disease. Jesus turned to the crowd and asked the question, "Who touched me?" and the disciples stated "we are in a crowd and you ask who touched you? The woman with the issue of blood fell at Jesus' feet and told him she touched his garment with the faith that she would be healed and Jesus said, "Daughter, you took a risk of faith, and now you're healed and whole. Live well, live blessed! Be healed of your plague."

The messages I want you to take away from this well-known bible story is there may come a time when you will be sick but you must have faith to see you through the illness. The woman with the issue of blood tried everything in her power to find a cure but it was only through God's power that she was immediately healed from her disease. The most important lesson to learn from the story is she had faith but her perseverance of making her way to Jesus and touching his garment also played a role in her healing. The woman with blood also "came clean" and told Jesus what she had done and in doing so Jesus sent her on to live a blessed life. **It is important to understand the more we depend on God completely, we will see our salvation through Him. This process will teach you how to love yourself as God loves you.**

A Healthy You

Taking care of your family is an honor and an extremely important gift. If you have ever flown on an airplane, the flight attendant will share with each passenger instructions to follow in the case of an emergency to ensure the safety of each passenger. The next statement advises parents traveling with children to secure themselves first and then care for the child. So in the same pattern, you must take care of yourself first before you can care for anyone else. Do you take care of everyone else and fail to make your health a top priority? How important is your health?

Answer the following questions to help assess your current health patterns:

- ✓ Do you eat food that nourishes your body and provides the right amount of nutrients and vitamins?

- ✓ Do you eat a good breakfast every morning such as oatmeal or an egg white omelet with fruit?
- ✓ Do you snack on fruit, vegetables or low fat yogurt?
- ✓ Do you eat a low carb lunch and dinner?
- ✓ Do you eat fast food meals 3-5 days per week?
- ✓ Do you cook meals at home?
- ✓ Do you eat late at night or happy hour restaurants?
- ✓ Do you participate in daily exercise?
- ✓ Do you sleep 7-8 hours every night?
- ✓ Do you schedule regular doctor visits to monitor your health?
- ✓ Do you have stress in your life?

As women we can take care of everyone else first and neglect our own health and well-being. Your assignment is to make your health a priority! Review the following health tips and put in the work for a healthy and better you!

<u>My Daily Personal Health Plan</u>

- ✓ Start your day in meditation with the word of God (this allows your spirit to be fed and starts your day with direction and purpose)
- ✓ Exercise in the morning (If you are able)

- ✓ Eat healthy (balanced breakfast, low carb lunch and dinner)
- ✓ Leave home in enough time to get to work to decrease the stress of being late
- ✓ Stay positive throughout the day
- ✓ Call a family member to see how they are doing or if they need anything
- ✓ Attend an activity for your child or another family member's child
- ✓ Participate in bible study throughout the week
- ✓ Volunteer your time to help someone
- ✓ Learn something new
- ✓ Walk after each meal
- ✓ Visit your doctor yearly or as needed
- ✓ Review all medication
- ✓ Spend time with family and friends
- ✓ Sleep for 8 hours
- ✓ Power down from all social media for 10 hours (this includes 8 hours of sleep)
- ✓ Take a vacation

- ✓ Read a book
- ✓ Laugh, Laugh, Laugh
- ✓ End the day with reflection and thanks to the Almighty

PERSONAL REFLECTION

1. What would your personal health plan look like?
2. What are some things you can do to center yourself spiritually or mentally?
3. What can you do to improve health and wellness individually and as a family?

HELPFUL STUDY

- ❖ Proverbs 3:7-8, "Trust God from the bottom of your heart; don't try to figure out everything on your own. Listen for God's voice in everything you do, everywhere you go; he's the one who will keep you on track. Don't assume that you know it all. Run to God! Run from evil! Your body will glow with health, your very bones will vibrate with life!"
- ❖ Proverbs 14:30, "A sound mind makes for a robust body, but runaway emotions corrode the bones."
- ❖ Luke 8:40-56, "And a woman was there who had been subject to bleeding for twelve years, but no one could heal her. She came up behind him and touched the edge

of his cloak, and immediately her bleeding stopped. "Who touched me?" Jesus asked, when they all denied it, Peter said, "Master, the people are crowding and pressing against you." But Jesus said, "Someone touched me; I know that power has gone out from me." Then the woman, seeing that she could not go unnoticed, came trembling and fell at his feet. In the presence of all the people, she told why she had touched him and how she had been instantly healed. Then he said to her, "Daughter, your faith has healed you. Go in peace."

- Ephesians 6:10-14, "Finally, be strong in the Lord and in his mighty power. Put on the full armor of God, so that you can take your stand against the devil's schemes. For our struggle is not against flesh and blood, but against the rulers, against the authorities, against the powers of this dark world and against the spiritual forces of evil in the heavenly realms. Therefore put on the full armor of God, so that when the day of evil comes, you may be able to stand your ground, and after you have done everything, to stand. Stand firm then, with the belt of truth buckled around your waist, with the breastplate of righteousness in place."

- 1st Peter 1:13-16, "So roll up your sleeves, put your mind in gear, be totally ready to receive the gift that's coming when Jesus arrives. Don't lazily slip back into those old grooves of evil, doing just what you feel like doing. You didn't know any better then; you do now. As obedient children, let yourselves be pulled into a way of life shaped by God's life, a life energetic and blazing with holiness. God said, "I am holy; you be holy."

Jewel: Compassionate

Proverbs 31: 20
"She's quick to assist anyone in need, reaches out to help the poor."

Do you have a mother-in-law? What is your relationship with her? Is it loving or is there room for growth and intimacy? When you follow the story of Ruth you are able to experience a loving relationship between a mother-in-law and her son's wives. It is through the love Ruth shows to her mother-in-law that we are able to experience the jewel of compassion.

Naomi and Ruth's Story

Naomi and her husband Elimelech moved from their homeland of Bethlehem to Moab with their two sons Mahlon and Chilion to avoid famine. While living in Moab, Elimelech unfortunately died and left Naomi a widower and a single mother. Naomi raised her two sons and each married a woman; Mahlon married Ruth and Chilion married Orpah. Naomi loved and mentored both of her daughters-in-law and because of this relationship a very close bond was built between the three women. Disaster fell to Naomi again and both of Naomi's sons died leaving Ruth and Orpah widows and Naomi without children.

The customs of this time allowed a childless widow to be married by her husband's brother to raise an heir for the deceased (Deut. 25:5-10). Naomi understood the custom and with both of her sons being deceased and as Naomi was not pregnant she could not offer her daughters-in-law any protection. So, Naomi encouraged her daughters-in-law to go back to their mothers so they could be married again and have children. Naomi's actions showed her thoughtfulness, compassion and love for her daughters-in-law.

Orpah chose to go back to her family but Ruth stayed with her mother-in-law. Ruth's decision to follow Naomi meant she would leave her homeland, culture, customs and traditions to live in foreign land to be with her mother-n-law. Ruth's compassion for Naomi was honored and Naomi was blessed by her decisions to be faithful. When Ruth and Naomi moved to their new home a respected man in the community named Boaz, married Ruth and bought the estate of Naomi. Ruth and Naomi are both great examples of two women who showed love and compassion for one another.

Compassionate Living

How often are you compassionate with your spouse or other people? When life is challenging do you attack and find blame? Do you blame your spouse's short comings or family background or environment? Do you show tenderness? Love? Kindness? Mercy? Christian compassion is when we understand that people are naturally flawed and yet we still show kindness and empathy through their faults and errors. This is the same compassion we expect others to show us in our time of need.

How can you practice compassionate living? First, in all things pray! When you pray you offer a spiritual sacrifice to God. This is a time you are petitioning God with your heart's desires and bringing your burdens, problems and stresses to the almighty. Mature Christians understand prayer is where you begin while young Christians call their friends or look to other sources for answers. The answers are always found in God's word.

Second, watch the words that pass through your lips because your mouth speaks the thoughts of your heart. Your words are a reflection of your heart and are then transmitted to the brain for memory. You do not want bitterness to rest in your heart because your words will reflect negative emotions. This is why it is so important to talk to God first because if you call your friends and speak negatively about your spouse then your friends will carry those same feelings and may not provide you with the best advice. Work on positive and supportive words because you will then begin to speak life!

Janine's Story

Janine was having challenges in her marriage and wanted her husband to spend more time with her and to be more communicative. Janine's husband would not go to counseling and refused to speak to the pastor. He was not going to have the pastor in his business and he was not going to pay a shrink to tell him how to live. Janine's husband shared with her that his father did not talk much and his parents' relationship was fine so there would be no more discussion about communication with him. Janine was hurt and looking for support so she contacted one of her friends from church. Janine's friend was a member of the women's ministry and was very friendly so she asked if they could meet for lunch. Janine explained how she felt very isolated and alone and did not know what to do; she shared very intimate information about her marriage, providing all the good and bad personality traits of Phillip. Janine's friend was a great listener and provided several scriptures for Janine to read and study. Three months passed and Janine felt the communication in her marriage was non-existent and Phillip was working late more nights than usual. All of a sudden Janine's sister took ill and she had to travel out of state for a week to care for her. Janine's sister recovered faster than expected so Janine returned from her trip early to surprise Phillip but to Janine's surprise Phillip had moved out of their bedroom and into the guest room. Janine was so hurt she just wanted to scream but she remembered her conversation with her friend around forgiveness and compassion. She pulled the scriptures related to compassion and forgiveness from her purse and read them several times. While Janine wasn't quite ready to tackle a conversation with her husband, she found the strength to pray and much needed comfort in her faith. After several weeks of fasting and praying unbeknownst to Janine, Phillip was listening to her morning prayers and study; after a time, Phillip approached Janine and said, "Baby can we talk?"

PERSONAL REFLECTION

1. Why is compassion so important?

2. Can you think of a time when your words were negative or hurtful? What made you speak this way? What can you do in the future to change this behavior?

3. What could have Janine done differently?

4. Have you ever been involved or witnessed this type of situation. What did you do?

5. What scriptures can provide comfort during this time of need?

Christian compassion is when we understand that people are naturally flawed and yet we still show kindness and empathy through their faults and errors. This is the same compassion we expect others to show us in our time of need.

HELPFUL STUDY

- Matthew 6:14-15, "In prayer there is a connection between what God does and what you do. You can't get forgiveness from God, for instance, without also forgiving others. If you refuse to do your part, you cut yourself off from God's part."

- Matthew 14:14, "When Jesus got the news, he slipped away by boat to an out-of-the-way place by himself. But unsuccessfully—someone saw him and the word got around. Soon a lot of people from the nearby villages walked around the lake to where he was. When he saw them coming, he was overcome with pity and healed their sick."

- Colossians 3:12-14, "So, chosen by God for this new life of love, dress in the wardrobe God picked out for you: compassion, kindness, humility, quiet strength, discipline. Be even-tempered, content with second place, quick to forgive an offense. Forgive as quickly and completely as the Master forgave you. And regardless of what else you put on, wear love. It's your basic, all-purpose garment. Never be without it."

Jewel: An Entrepreneurial Spirit And Future Planning

Proverbs 31: 21, 22 and 24

"She is not afraid of snow for her household, for all her household is clothed with scarlet. She makes her own clothing, and dresses in colorful linens and silks. She makes linen garments and sells them, and supplies sashes for the merchants."

Miranda always had a flair for applying the best make-up dating back to when she played with dolls. Miranda's mother allowed her to watch when she put on her make-up in the morning and on occasions even let Miranda put a little bit of rouge on her cheeks, too. When Miranda was in high school she would always touch up her make-up before class and if there was a girl in the bathroom who needed help, she would gladly try to fix them up without being late for class. After high school, Miranda did not go to college because she just didn't have the money, but she was able to find a job at a clothing store that paid well. Miranda still had friends and family members call her for make-up tips and paid her to do their make-up for special occasions. On one occasion Miranda was applying make-up on a woman from her church and the woman told her, "Miranda, you have missed your calling and this should be your business. You should market yourself and do this full time; you are gifted!" Miranda had heard this message before but this time she received it and decided it was time for her to get serious and start her own business. Miranda told her family of her plan to start a business, her company name and how she was going to move forward. Miranda took a class for managing your own business, made business cards and started "Make-up for You" that day. Miranda worked hard and applied make-up at any event or home where she was contracted in the first two years. This meant Miranda missed family functions, worked 60-hour weeks and took evening classes to learn new techniques in the make-up business. It was hard, but Miranda could not believe the success of her company. Within two years, she was applying make-up for entertainers who came to her city and she had just received a two-year contract to apply make-up for a television show. Miranda was able to leave her day job because she doubled her salary with "Make-Up for You" and was now a full time entrepreneur. As Miranda entered the fifth year of "Make-Up for You" she opened a store in the mall and had several employees training under her, while continuing to travel to most awards show as one of the most requested make-up artists.

Individuality

The entrepreneur jewel is about listening to God's word and being strong enough to stand alone if it is in conflict with the crowd. It is knowing that God has called you for a certain task, understanding you have been called and moving into action to do the work of what you were called to do. It is being able to work independently and take risks because you are following a plan of action.

The first action you must take in the entrepreneur jewel is to listen for God's voice. Listening requires your effort to hear God's voice, your action to understand his message and your ability to apply what you have heard and learned. My children know my voice because we communicate often and in many different ways. As they are now young adults, my conversations have moved to a place of support and advisement as they tackle young adult decisions. My young adult children call my husband and myself to gain a different perspective or to review their options based on their current situation. They call us because they have a trusting relationship with us and know we have their best interest in all situations. If you do not have a relationship with God then how will you know when he is talking to you? How will you build a relationship with the Almighty if you don't spend time with him to hear his voice? How will you know to avoid a challenging situation or to move swiftly to another if you are unable to decipher his voice and plan for you?

The second action in the entrepreneur jewel is knowing what you have been called to do and to persevere. There will be times when you may not feel as if your hard work will pay off or provide the intended outcome you expected. Miranda heard the message to start a business and it took over two years of sacrifices, hard work and perseverance to see her dreams become a reality. Perseverance teaches us patience, how to exercise self-control and how to live by faith. As Hebrews 11:1 states, "*the fundamental fact of existence is that this trust in God, this faith, is the firm foundation under everything that makes life worth living. It's our handle on what we can't see. The act of faith is what distinguished our ancestors, set them above the crowd.*"

The third action of the entrepreneur jewel is self-control which is shown through moderation and self-restraint. Miranda worked 60-hour weeks and spent her evenings taking classes to improve her business and make-up techniques. Based on this schedule, Miranda did not have much time for personal enjoyment or leisurely activities; she had to operate from a place of moderation and self-restraint. When you are called to God's plan your time may look different going forward compared to the past. You will spend more time in study, building your business, or creating something that has never been done before. You must sacrifice to support your destiny.

The fourth action of the entrepreneur jewel is patience which Merriam-Wester defines as, "A person's ability to wait something out or endure something tedious, without getting riled up". Your destiny may not happen overnight and in many cases takes years to see the benefits which is why patience is so important. When you plant a seed it takes time for the seed to grow and roots to develop for the beautiful flower that will bloom in the final stage. Patience allows us to live and grow in the process before the final product is revealed. If you move too fast, you may miss an important stage so take your time to learn everything you need to know so you are prepared for your future.

Perseverance teaches us patience, how to exercise self-control and how to live by faith.

PERSONAL REFLECTION

1. When and how do you listen to God's voice?

2. Has there been a time in your life when you have had to persevere? When and what did you do?

3. Have you had to exhibit self-control? What circumstances lead you to exhibit self-control?

4. Do exhibit patience? What areas in your life need patience?

5. Are you able to be independent in God's word? What can get in the way of following his plan for your life?

HELPFUL STUDY

- Romans 5:3-5, " There's more to come: We continue to shout our praise even when we're hemmed in with troubles, because we know how troubles can develop passionate patience in us, and how that patience in turn forges the tempered steel of virtue, keeping us alert for whatever God will do next. In alert expectancy such as this, we're never left feeling shortchanged. Quite the contrary—we can't round up enough containers to hold everything God generously pours into our lives through the Holy Spirit!"

- 2nd Peter 1:5-9, "So don't lose a minute in building on what you've been given, complementing your basic faith with good character, spiritual understanding, alert discipline, passionate patience, reverent wonder, warm friendliness, and generous love, each dimension fitting into and developing the others. With these qualities active and growing in your lives, no grass will grow under your feet, no day will pass without its reward as you mature in your experience of our Master Jesus. Without these qualities you can't see what's right before you, oblivious that your old sinful life has been wiped off the books."

- Ecclesiastes 7:8, "Endings are better than beginnings. Sticking to it is better than standing out."

Jewel: Married To A Leader

Proverbs 31:23

"Her husband is greatly respected when he deliberates with the city fathers."

Mr. Samuel Livingston served his country for over 20 years through two tours of duty then retired from military service when he was 40 years old. Samuel met Tracy Lynn through a friend and they married one year to the day of meeting. Samuel and Tracey were both the same age and had a very mature relationship, producing one son named Ethan. Samuel had nothing but time to spend with Ethan and took him along everywhere, to the barbershop every Saturday morning, to the corner store for bread and milk and to the gas station each week. When Ethan's friends came to the house, Samuel became a surrogate father to them and spent many hours providing guidance and stories of his experience in life while they visited Ethan at their home. Samuel tried to teach Ethan how to be a man based on his simple belief, "Honor and respect all that has been given to you because it can be removed at any time". When Ethan was 12 and getting bullied by the boys down the street while he walked home from school, Samuel started to walk with Ethan to let the boys know his son was not alone. Samuel also wanted to get to know the boys and walk with them as well. The boys started to come down the street and spend time with Samuel and eventually became friends with Ethan. After Ethan graduated from high school and left home to pursue his life, many of his friends still stopped by the house to check on Samuel and his wife. As Samuel looked back over his life, he was extremely proud of his time in the service, his family and his community involvement. When Samuel and Tracey married they did not believe they would ever have children at their age, but they had been blessed with Ethan. Samuel promised himself when Ethan was born to be the best father for Ethan as long as he lived. At age 86, Samuel had kept his promise to his son and was blessed to have supported many other young men in his family and neighborhood.

Male Leadership

Elder men have, as they say, "been there" and "done that," which allows them to not be moved by "fleeting fits of fancy" or the whims of a new fad. When you encounter a group of respected elder men, you will see them reason through issues that arise and spend time looking for solutions. Elder men are wise based on their years of experience and how they have lived their lives, which enables them to provide historical perspective, insight and personal reflection around most topics. When a man is respected in his community he is described as one who takes care of his business, his family, and a man who fears God.

A leader is defined as a person who leads or commands a group, organization or country. A few words to describe a leader are chief, CEO, manager, father, authority figure and protector. Does this mean that your spouse has to lead a company or be the President of the United States to be a leader? Absolutely not, because a CEO of a Fortune 500 company has the same requirements as the male CEO of the family and they both share the same characteristics. The characteristics of a male leader can be found in 1 Timothy 3: 2-7:

2 A leader must be well-thought of, committed to his wife, cool and collected, accessible, and hospitable.

3 He must know what he is talking about not be over fond of wine, not pushy, but gentle, not thin- skinned, not money hungry.

4 He must handle his own affairs well, attentive to his own children and have their respect.

5 For if someone is unable to handle his own affairs, how can he take care of God's church?

6 He must not be a new believer, lest the position go to his head and the Devil trip him up.

7 Outsiders must think well of him, or else the Devil will figure out a way to lure him into his trap.

Good Fruit

As you review the characteristics of a leader how will you know a leader when see one? Matthew 7:20 states, "Thus, by their fruits, you will recognize them." When you pick fruit from a tree there is a process. You look at the color, outward appearance, character traits and texture. In order to pick the best quality fruit you have to further examine the fruit in greater detail looking for flaws or imperfections that can compromise the taste of the fruit. This process takes time.

If you are from the city and have never visited a farm then your experience with fruit will take place at the grocery store or farmers market. The process will be the same, when you view fruit at the market or grocery store most people will take their time and inspect the fruit to ensure it is ripe and the best possible fruit to eat. Most people will determine the type of fruit to eat based on the condition of the fruit, how well it satisfies the pallet or if it is low hanging fruit and is the easiest to pick or choose. You do not want to eat bitter fruit (picked to soon, underdeveloped) or fruit that is past its shelf life (stayed on the tree too long, rotten) because it will not satisfy your experience.

The way we view the quality and characteristics of the fruit is parallel to the leadership qualities of a man. I don't have to find out the qualities and characteristics of a man from other people because I will be able to observe them in his everyday walk of life. Keep in mind, all fruit upon examination will have some flaws, but you have to identify the character traits through deep examination, experience and prayer. In choosing good fruit I am looking for the characteristics defined in 1 Timothy knowing that there is no perfect fruit. There is only fruit that has the best qualities. Some fruit will have soft spots and bruises, but the quality and characteristics are above reproach. Which simply means when someone shows you who they are....***believe them.*** The fruit is the fruit. Many people purchase questionable fruit and try to remove the questionable parts to create a new fruit or ignore the taste and quality. You are not creating a new fruit but destroying a portion of the original fruit to make it better. The fruit is still the same. Take the time to observe, study and learn the fruit before picking to determine if the fruit is acceptable to you. Many people ignore the quality of the fruit based on potential, style of dress or financial status and when this happens you never have a clear picture of the fruit.

The same is true for relationships, you must take the time to make sure your potential mate is the "right fruit" for you and to ensure you are successful in this area I recommend you follow the Q-TIP plan:

Q - TIP

Q = Ask many **Q**uestions.
T = **T**ake **T**ime to listen and get to know your potential mate.
I = Gather **I**nformation.
P = **P**atience with **P**rocess and look for **P**atterns.

What questions should you ask when getting to know someone? The following list of questions I asked my husband, and some he asked me, over 25 years ago and they are still relevant today. I have added a few questions based on the addition of social media and our ever changing society. The following questions will provide you with relevant data to see if this person will be a "fit" or the right "fruit" for you:

1. What do you like to do for fun?

2. What high school did you attend and what year did you graduate? What college did you attend and what year did you graduate? What happened if you didn't graduate?

3. What has been your work experience?

4. Who are your parents? Are your parents married or divorced? What is their story? Do you have siblings? Where are you in the line-up of siblings?

5. If you are a male, describe how you feel about your mother. What is your current relationship with

your mother? What is your current relationship with your father? (Very important questions)

6. Are you currently employed? Do you like to work?

7. What is your family medical history?

8. Have you ever dated someone of the same gender?

9. Have you made a gender change from what is listed on your birth certificate?

10. Do you have children and how many? Do you pay child support? Have you had to work through the penal system for child support?

11. What is your relationship with your child's mother?

12. Have you been married before and how many times?

13. What are your plans for the next 5, 10, 15, 20, 25 years?

14. Have you ever dated someone outside of your race? What were the positive aspects you gained from the relationship?

15. What is your dream job?

16. Do you have a spiritual foundation?

17. What is your FICO score?

18. Have you ever owned a home?

19. Have you ever been diagnosed with an STD?

20. Do you take medication?

21. Do you like to travel?

22. Have you ever had surgery?

23. Are you truthful?

24. How would your family members and friends describe you?

25. How was your father's relationship with your mother?

26. Have you ever been a perpetrator or victim of abuse?

27. What is your everyday language?

28. Do you take prescription or illegal drugs?

29. Do you drink socially, daily, in excess and how often?

To know someone's fruit, you must take the time through observation, study and interaction to learn their characteristics. Only time will allow you to see people for who they really are and if they will bend, break or with stand the pressures of life.

PERSONAL REFLECTION

1. What are the characteristics in 1 Timothy that your spouse possesses? List them.
2. How can you support your spouse in the areas that he does not possess?
3. What do other men say about your spouse?
4. What characteristics have you missed or observed while inspecting fruit?

HELPFUL STUDY

- ❖ Proverbs 24:7, "Wisdom is too high for fools; in the assembly at the gate they must not open their mouths."
- ❖ Deuteronomy 16:18, "Appoint judges and officials for each of your tribes in every town the Lord your God is giving you, and they shall judge the people fairly."
- ❖ Ruth 4:1-2, "Meanwhile Boaz went up to the town gate and sat down there just as the guardian-redeemer he had mentioned came along. Boaz said, "Come over here, my friend, and sit down." So he went over and sat down. Boaz took ten of the elders of the town and said, "Sit here," and they did so."

Jewel: Not *Swayed* By Circumstance

Proverbs 31:25
"She is clothed with strength and dignity; she can laugh at the days to come."

Shelley graduated from college and was accepted into a master's program through a program designed to recruit teachers to a northern Midwestern area. Shelley was excited for her new beginning because the program took care of her student loans and she had decided to let go of an on and off again college romance. Truly, it was time for a new beginning in her life. Shelley could never have anticipated the extremely frigid weather before her arrival, but eventually she adjusted to the many winter activities which took place from November through March. Shelley stayed in the area for over 18 years and seriously dated three men during this time. Each time, each man turned out not to be the "one." Shelley did not like to share her personal business with others so when asked who she was dating, she always characterized the name with a number. There was "The First", with his meticulous style and everything must be defined personality; "The Second", the business man who was so accommodating and nice; and "The Third", the corporate climber, who enjoyed the good time but exited the ride when Shelley announced she was pregnant with their child. Shelley decided to raise the child and "The Third" assisted Shelley financially but stayed true to not having a relationship with his daughter. Shelley met "The Fourth" through a mutual friend while they both were on a trip in another county. They dated for one year long distance and a second year once "The Fourth" was able to move to the states through a visa. "The Fourth" accepted Shelley's daughter, respected her (as was custom in his culture) and proposed to Shelley and asked her to be his queen. "The Fourth" and Shelley were set to marry at the justice of the peace Friday at 4 p.m. so Shelley went to work and was supposed to work until 1:30 and then she would take the rest of the day off to meet "The Fourth" at the court house. Shelley's students started to question if she was going to get married because she was still at the school at 2 p.m. Shelley stayed married to "The Fourth" for seven years until the marriage unraveled and they had a very bitter divorce. "The Fourth" tried to hide all of his business assets in another country and told the presiding divorce judge that he moved to the states to marry his wife and Shelley was abandoning him and he should be compensated for his pain and suffering. Shelley could not believe the situation she was in at her age and was completely embarrassed and hurt by the entire situation. Shelley, a divorcee? She was too smart for this and what would people think of her? Shelley was so angry with herself because she knew she should not have married "The Fourth" in the first place, and only agreed because he had asked. Shelley did not believe there would ever be another opportunity for marriage so she accepted his offer out of fear and not love. When the marriage was in a very ugly space (Shelley was living upstairs in the house and "The Fourth" was living downstairs) an acquaintance called her and shared a job opportunity in another state and said Shelley should apply which she did. She received a job offer from the company and the next thing she knew, her friends and relatives helped her pack up her things and she moved to another state, her next new beginning. With Kyla in college and as a fairly young empty-nester, after the divorce Shelley vowed she would never marry again, for she had learned the hard lesson that divorce is ugly and financially draining as she lost her pension in the divorce settlement. But she learned that peace of mind was priceless, so she began to let go of the bitterness that was eating her whole. Several months after the divorce, Shelley went out with friends and met a man named Ryan who was nothing like any of the previous men she had dated. Ryan was a great father, his grown children adored him and he loved spending time with Shelley. Shelley married Ryan at a church, with a reception and because she truly loved

Ryan, they both wanted to make sure God was in the center of their relationship.

Mirror, Mirror on the Wall

When you look in the mirror who looks back at you each morning? Is it your younger self still trying to find her way? Is it the mature woman who has experienced life and has the scars to show for her travels? Is it the "I just can't get my life together" person looking back at you? I think the most important question is "Who is the woman God sees in me?"

How do you start your day? Do you pray before you get out of bed? Do you have an exercise routine and workout at home or at a gym in the morning? Do you complete or start laundry? Do you turn on the television and watch the news? Whenever you start or finish your daily routine, you will eventually make your way to the bathroom to prepare for the day. Most bathrooms are equipped with a mirror to provide a reflection of how we look. I use the mirror to look to see if my make-up has been applied correctly. I can check to see if my hair is out of place. I can look in the mirror and assess my overall presentation to the world. I can check to make sure my clothes match and I am not wearing one blue sock and a black sock at the same time. However, these checks are just superficial...we need to go deeper!

Activity

Find a mirror and look at yourself. Look at your face, look at your body, look inside of who you are and then describe what you see and how you feel about yourself. List your talents and gifts. Find adjectives to describe yourself, like Marvelous Mary or Serious Stephanie. Describe who you are on the inside and outside.

As I look through my mirror I see many different things – I first start with the surface areas:

- Is my overall appearance neat and clean?
- Did I apply my make-up appropriately?
- Do my clothes look presentable? Ironed?
- Did I get enough rest or do I look tired?

When I go deeper and look on the inside where no one can see –

- Will I measure up today?
- Am I smart enough?
- Will people see the person that I try desperately to hide?

Many times we avoid looking into the mirror because the reflection in the mirror is not always pretty. While the mirror can't reflect the internal things we mask so others can't see, we know what is hiding behind the true reflection. As you look in the mirror and see this woman, was she:

- Abused, verbally and/or physically
- Fat, skinny, odd or perfectly shaped
- Inadequate or adequate enough
- Unattractive or too attractive
- Smart enough
- Too verbal (talks to much)
- Promiscuous
- Someone who sleeps with married men or an adulteress
- Someone who cohabitates with a man without benefit of clergy
- Different

- A divorcee
- Married and unhappy
- Barren, unable to have children
- Someone who has too many children and can barely handle one
- Abandoned
- Nasty in language and to people
- Fired
- A gossip
- A person who uses profanity, curses
- A person with a bad attitude
- Worthy enough to have a good man, someone who treats me well and does not use me for sex or money
- Do I only see my disease: diabetes, cancer, lupus, depression, mental health issues, thyroid issues, wheel-chair bound, down syndrome, autism, HIV and or AIDS, herpes, chlamydia, psoriasis, eczema

After today, when you start to think these thoughts, as you look in the mirror, I want you to know the voice you hear is not yours.

John 10:10 states, *"A thief is only there to steal and kill and destroy. I came so they can have real and eternal life, more and better life than they ever dreamed of."* The enemy wants to destroy you because if he can conquer your mind then he can try to stop you from becoming the Woman God has called you to be and destroy your peace and well-being in the Queendom. He is going to speak to your mind and tell you that ---you can't change, your mother and your father are this way and you will be also or you can't make it out of your situation and are not worthy of greatness. This is why the second sentence is so important:

"I came so they can have real and eternal life, more and better life than they ever dreamed of"

God is our father and just like my biological father told me every morning that I was his morning glory, then we are God's morning glory, too. We are always enough because He died on the cross so that we could be enough!

God does not expect us to get our self-worth from the world, our friends, our jobs, our careers or our family....I only have to be concerned with HOW GOD views me. I know that He loves me unconditionally! When I look in the mirror I don't have to concern myself with the physical reflection of the mirror because GOD only sees Himself in me.

This becomes our walk of faith. Do you trust GOD in His timing? Do you trust Him enough to wait until He feels you are ready for the right career, spouse, children or cure for your disease?

When you are clothed in strength and honor and smile at the future, you are exhibiting the jewel of not being swayed by your circumstance and this is modeled through:

1. Spending enough time in the word of God to strengthen your everyday walk.

2. Praying daily for understanding.

3. Understanding you are not in control but following God's will and path.

4. Having faith.

When tough situations walk into your life you are not swayed by the storm because you put your faith in God. When you put your faith in God and not in your own ability to solve problems then you will be able to stand firmly in the storm and know that you will be delivered in God's time. He will protect you and allow you to share your story (testimony) with others about how He kept you and delivered you from the storm. You will smile while you tell the story.

PERSONAL REFLECTION

1. Have you ever experienced a situation where you felt you could not overcome? What happened and how did you handle the experience?

2. Do you blame yourself for past mistakes? How do you recover from past mistakes?

3. What life experiences have been the most challenging and the most rewarding?

4. What will you do moving forward to not be swayed by your circumstance? How will you determine your success?

HELPFUL STUDY

❖ Ephesians 4:20-24, "But that's no life for you. You learned Christ! My assumption is that you have paid careful attention to him, been well instructed in the truth precisely as we have it in Jesus. Since, then, we do not have the excuse of ignorance, everything—and I do mean everything—connected with that old way of life has to go. It's rotten through and through. Get rid of it! And then take on an entirely new way of life—a God-fashioned life, a life renewed from the inside and working itself into your conduct as God accurately reproduces his character in you."

- 1 Timothy 2:8-10, "Since prayer is at the bottom of all this, what I want mostly is for men to pray—not shaking angry fists at enemies but raising holy hands to God. And I want women to get in there with the men in humility before God, not primping before a mirror or chasing the latest fashions but doing something beautiful for God and becoming beautiful doing it."

- 1 Peter 5:5-7, "And you who are younger must follow your leaders. But all of you, leaders and followers alike, are to be down to earth with each other, for—God has had it with the proud, but takes delight in just plain people. So be content with who you are, and don't put on airs. God's strong hand is on you; he'll promote you at the right time. Live carefree before God; he is most careful with you."

- 2 Corinthians 1:8-10, "We don't want you in the dark, friends, about how hard it was when all this came down on us in Asia province. It was so bad we didn't think we were going to make it. We felt like we'd been sent to death row that it was all over for us. As it turned out, it was the best thing that could have happened. Instead of trusting in our own strength or wits to get out of it, we were forced to trust God totally—not a bad idea since he's the God who raises the dead! And he did it, rescued us from certain doom. And he'll do it again, rescuing us as many times as we need rescuing. You and your prayers are part of the rescue operation—I don't want you in the dark about that either."

Jewel: Wise

Proverbs 31:26
"When she speaks she has something worthwhile to say, and she always says it kindly."

Candice could not wait to graduate from high school and move from the small town where she had spent the last 18 years of her life. Candice was determined she was going to make it and get a college degree. She had two teachers who said she was really smart and had potential; her English teacher Mrs. Ray and her Science teacher Mr. Candoodle. Candice's mom, Darlene, worked extremely hard at a factory job every day during the second shift from 4 p.m. to midnight so she could clean houses during the day. Even with both jobs, Darlene never had enough money to pay the bills or buy food to eat. If it were not for eating breakfast and lunch at school Candice did not know how she would eat every day. When her school started to offer meals for the students staying after school Candice made sure she was connected to an after-school program so she could eat everyday while at school. Darlene had taught Candice how to make meals stretch on the weekend for the family, which included a brother, and somehow they made it work. Darlene was from the same small town and graduated from the same high school as Candice. She married the star lacrosse player, Aaron, who dreamed of playing professional lacrosse. Aaron's plans changed when he injured himself in college tryouts which brought him back home. Aaron was bitter about not getting the break he deserved and blamed Darlene for tying him down with two kids and a family. Darlene divorced Aaron and took him to court for back child support because she needed help raising their son and daughter. Aaron decided he was not going to work and give his money to the system so he stopped working completely and never provided any money nor did he spend time with his kids. When Candice's teacher started talking to her about applying for college, Candice did not believe college was for her but then she realized through her teachers that a college education is the one way to free herself from repeating the same life as her mother having to struggle from paycheck to paycheck. Candice made sure her grades were good so that if she qualified for any scholarships nothing would deter her from getting a college degree. Candice was determined not to live everyday worrying about where her next meal was coming from or worry about if she was going to walk in the house and the lights were going to be shut off from insufficient funds or no funds at all. When Candice received her acceptance letter to several universities, she was thrilled but Darlene was not and wanted Candice to stay at home and get a job at the factory and help her clean homes. Darlene said she needed to focus on the real world and stop wasting her time on dreams that would not come true. Rich people attended college and she was not rich and college was not for her daughter.

Candice was not going to let anyone get in her way of following her dreams to get to college and if it meant moving away from her family to get her college degree and better herself then she would have to do what was necessary because she was not going give up on her dream.

Wisdom

Have you ever been in the presence of wise women? What made them wise? Did you base your opinion from their words and or actions? Have these women always been wise or did they develop their wisdom over time? Giftsrest.com describes someone who has the gift of wisdom as "having divine strength or ability to understand and to bring clarity to situations and circumstances often through applying the truths of scripture in a practical way." Would you go to a "reality television show" to gain advice on how to have a successful marriage? Would you try to gain wisdom from your friends who are experiencing the same hardships or problems as you? Often times we gain wisdom from watching others and learning from their mistakes but most times we learn the hard knocks of life through personal experience. We must learn to listen to wisdom and act accordingly. This means we can't hang on to our past!

Lot's Wife

What do we know about the story of Lot and his wife? Lot was a relative of Abraham who was chosen by God to be the heir of God's unconditional covenant or promise to his people. We know God visited Abraham with angels and told him they were going to the cities of Sodom and Gomorrah to destroy them. Abraham asked God if he would destroy Sodom and Gomorrah if there were 40 decent people living in the cities and God answers, "No". Abraham then asked if there were 20 decent people and God answers, "No". The Lord continued and apparently there were not even 10 decent people living in the cities of Sodom and Gomorrah. So God sent two angels in human form to take Lot and his family safely from Sodom.

Sodom was a cultural and sophisticated city that was unquestionably corrupt. We don't know why Lot chose to live in an immoral city with his family, but he did. Lot's wife enjoyed and loved the city because her friends and family were there. We need to reflect on Lot's wife current situation. She was able to witness a miracle by being in the presence of angels and participating in the rescue of her family. She was privy to information about what was going to happen to the city just by being married to Lot, who some would describe as a righteous man. If this story happened today we would say Lot's wife had insider information to assist her with the decision to leave the city. If we were watching the story of Lot's wife at a movie theater, this would be the time when people would yell from their seats toward the screen, "Pack your bags and go! Run, save yourself and your family!" The problem is Lot's wife does not want to leave! Her heart is with her family, the city she loves and everything familiar to her. As Lot's family is being rescued from Sodom they are given specific and clear instructions not to look back but Lot's wife lacked wisdom and turned to look back at her beloved city and became a pillar of salt.

Some mistakes are minor and have minimal consequences while others have life or death consequences such as Lot's wife. God gave Lot's family an opportunity to live but Lot's wife was too consumed with what she was losing instead of what she was gaining. The treasure of her heart was back in Sodom and she did not understand her heart was deceived. What areas from your past are you still holding on to and don't want to leave? There are people and relationships you should leave but you continue to stay. It could be your best friend is negative and detrimental to your well-being but your mothers are friends and they both continually put pressure on you to keep in contact and be friends even though the relationship is not good for you. If you continue in this one-sided friendship, then you are still hanging on to your past. You may have to sit down with your mother and explain you care for your friend but you are living in a positive space and your former friend does not fit into your new equation. The season of the relationship ended and it is time to move into your next season. We must stop holding on to things God has called us to leave.

We are to be faithful in Him and follow the steps he has ordered us to walk without fear. Fear of change, fear of loss, fear of the unknown and fear of our potential, fear of not being in control, fear of loving someone that you know does not love you back, fear of being unwanted, fear of rejection, fear of the person leaving you for another, fear of starting over with someone new, fear of being alone, fear of the man God called for you never showing up, fear of loving yourself and the fear of submission to God. The list can go on and on but understand fear can and does stop our growth and can get in the way of our peace and future. ***Fear will make us travel a road that was never intended for us to avoid the fear of the unknown which is what God has planned for us.***

In all areas of our lives we must use prayer and wisdom as we make decisions. Like Lot's wife, if we take our eyes off the prize and get lured into a world of smoking mirrors and glass then we will never walk into our destiny.

PERSONAL REFLECTION

1. Are you still hanging on to your past? Why?

2. Can you identify the obstacles that prevent you from seeing your future?

3. How is your heart deceived?

4. What causes you to continue to be attracted to the past or the things you need to leave behind?

HELPFUL STUDY

- ❖ Genesis 19:15-17, 26 and Luke 17:32, "At break of day, the angels pushed Lot to get going, "Hurry. Get your wife and two daughters out of here before it's too late and you're caught in the punishment of the city. Lot was dragging his feet. The men grabbed Lot's arm, and the arms of his wife and daughters—God was so merciful to them!—and dragged them to safety outside the city. When they had them outside, Lot was told, "Now run for your life! Don't look back! Don't stop anywhere on the plain—run for the hills or you'll be swept away." "But Lot's wife looked back and turned into a pillar of salt."

- Luke 17:32, "Remember Lot's wife."

- Esther 5:7-8, "Esther answered, "Here's what I want. If the king favors me and is pleased to do what I desire and ask, let the king and Haman come again tomorrow to the dinner that I will fix for them. Then I'll give a straight answer to the king's question."

- Ephesians 4:29, "Watch the way you talk. Let nothing foul or dirty come out of your mouth. Say only what helps, each word a gift."

Jewel: Kindness

Proverbs 31:26
"When she speaks she has something worthwhile to say, and she always says it kindly."

Taylor could not wait for Byron to get home because she was going to give him a piece of her mind. Taylor was tired of him not cleaning up after himself leaving his socks around the house and putting plates on the counter without rinsing them off and putting them in the dishwasher. Bryon had another thing coming if he thought she was going to be his maid! It was bad enough that his mother had not raised him to take care of himself, she washed all his clothes and ironed them for Byron. He wasn't willing to do anything around the apartment and when Taylor would complain, Byron would just walk out the room and say "Momma is a good woman and she did it so you can too, baby." Well I am not going to be his baby tonight and I have a word for Mr. Byron and his mother, Taylor thought. As soon as Byron walks in the door it will be World War III and IV and if he brings up his momma again, then I am going to tell Byron how his mother did a poor job of raising him and that she raised a momma's boy. Taylor knew this was going to be a bullseye hit to Byron because Byron loved his mother and Taylor could not say anything about his mother without Byron getting upset. Byron's dad had died when he was 11 and Byron's mother raised him and his younger brother. Byron always talked about how his mother had sacrificed for the family and told Taylor that his mother was his number one woman and it would take a special woman to take her place. Taylor felt honored when Byron asked her to marry him, but she did not realize all the work that Byron required and Taylor felt betrayed and angry that she had to work just like Byron and then come home to cook, clean and do laundry while Byron read the paper or watched television. Today was the last day and Taylor had been rehearsing all the things she was going to say about Byron and if she was unable to get a rise out of him then she would bring up how successful his brother was and then let the fireworks begin! When Taylor had her last thought, Byron walked through the door and walked to Taylor and said, "Hey baby how was your day?" and tried to kiss Taylor but she moved her face and said, "How was my day? What you should ask me is how did I enjoy picking up after you today Byron?" or maybe "Do I look like your mother?" Byron did not want to hear Taylor talk about his mother and he was tired from work but if she wanted an argument tonight she was going to get one and it may mean he would have to go to his mom's house tonight because it was the only place Byron could get any peace.

Tone, Tongue and Temperament

Would the people in your home describe you as kind and loving? Being kind is easy for some and extremely challenging for others. I like to call this jewel 3-T because it is about our tone, tongue and temperament.

3 – T
Tone, Tongue and Temperament

There are many scriptures that address our mouths or more specific the words that we speak. The old children's rhyme stating sticks and stones will break my bones but names will never hurt me is so untrue. Words do hurt and have lasting implications.

A Fair Fight

A kind woman is so important because it sets the tone and temperament of the home. There was a time early in my marriage when I was irritated at Patrick for something he had done. When he got home from work he could tell by my body language and tone of voice that I was still unhappy. During the day I had thought about how I was going to tell Patrick about himself. I had elevated my attack status to sniper mode and my plan was to annihilate Patrick using my best weapon...words. In any war, there is a strategy to win and at this time in my marriage I felt my words would provide the most power (remember, I was young). When you have an intimate relationship with someone, you know their successes but you also know their shortcomings. I knew the exact topic to use and the words to describe his shortcomings to make a bullseye hit. After two good days of war we finally called a truce, but the casualty of this war left some deep scars and took some time to heal. We both had to learn how to fight fairly and eventually not fight at all. I had to learn how to temper my tongue and be kind to Patrick when I was irritated with him. This shift in my war strategy was challenging because it had nothing to do with Patrick and everything to do with me. I had to make a shift, not for Patrick, but for myself. There is a time and place for everything and starting or continuing a heated discussion as soon as you get home does not show wisdom. Proverbs 21:9 states it is, "Better to live alone in a tumbledown shack than share a mansion with a nagging spouse."

If your home is stressful and negative then your spouse will want to be anywhere but home. Kindness is so important because we are showing a temperament of being sweet and loving. When you are kind, you are adaptable or amenable to the needs of others. You want to serve to meet the needs of someone else. To be kind at home means you will represent a willingness to serve and to change in order to meet the needs of your spouse. This is how we gain respect and influence from our spouses because we are able to exhibit kindness through our words and actions which produces a loving environment. The following examples will provide you with sample acts of kindness you can use for the next 30 days:

1. Wake up and say Good Morning, I love you.
2. Pray with your spouse daily. (It is one of the most intimate conversations)
3. Start your day with bible study together.
4. Pray for your spouse daily.
5. Tell your spouse you are thankful they are in your life.
6. Text your spouse during the day to say you are thinking of them and use Bitmojis. (bitmoji.com-free app)
7. Make breakfast before he leaves for work.
8. Bring lunch to his job.
9. Put a positive note in his pocket or lunch.
10. Text a positive scripture.
11. Have his favorite meal ready for dinner.
12. Have a picnic at home or in the park.

13. Schedule date night once a week.

14. Schedule a visit with his family.

15. Pack some snacks for him during the day.

16. Draw a bath with soothing music at night before bed for relaxation.

17. Be quick to listen and slow to speak.

18. Look for solutions in all things and not blame.

19. Let him walk in the house and sit for 15 minutes to make the transition from work to home.

20. Get his favorite concert, sport or movie tickets.

21. Give a card with 25 things you love about him.

22. Have quiet time together for 15 minutes each night.

23. Say something positive about him each day.

24. Tell him he looks good in your favorite outfit.

25. Have him schedule time to do something with his friends.

26. Invite his friends over to your home to hang out with him.

27. Rent or stream his favorite movie and watch together.

28. Get a subscription to a men's magazine.

29. Massage his shoulders at night to release tension.

30. Give him the opportunity to just talk while you listen to his day.

PERSONAL REFLECTION

1. How often do you observe acts of kindness in your home or work environment?

2. Why is kindness so important?

3. Have you exhibited kindness to your spouse or other? What was their response or reaction?

HELPFUL STUDY

- ❖ Psalms 34:13, "Guard your tongue from profanity and no more lying through your teeth."

- ❖ Psalms 52:1-4, "Why do you brag of evil, "Big Man"? God's mercy carries the day. You scheme catastrophe; your tongue cuts razor-sharp, artisan in lies. You love evil more than good, you call black white. You love malicious gossip, you foul-mouth."

- ❖ Psalms 64:2-4, "Don't let them find me— the conspirators out to get me, using their tongues as weapons, flinging poison words, poison-tipped arrow-words. They shoot from ambush, shoot without warning, not caring who they hit."

- Psalms 120:2, "Deliver me from the liars, God! They smile so sweetly but lie through their teeth."

- Proverbs 21:23, "Watch your words and hold your tongue; you'll save yourself a lot of grief."

Jewel: Duty-Conscious

Proverbs 31:27

"She keeps an eye on everyone in her household, and keeps them all busy and productive."

Jillian was promoted to a manager position after working at her current organization for the past three years. The process to become a manager was challenging but after the third interview she was hired in the position. Jillian received many congratulatory emails and cards from co-workers who felt she was the right person for the job. Jillian took her job seriously and made sure she spoke to all staff members that she came in contact with daily. She collaborated with her team and worked diligently with the corporate partners to ensure their level of service was always professional and timely. Jillian was punctual and timely with reports and always took the time to have her teammates provide input on any document representing the department. When Jillian's boss asked her what made her the most qualified applicant for the job she described her love for the company, her ability to work in teams and her belief in striving for excellence in her work. She was so happy about her new job because everything she said in her job interview was true and the opportunity to manage a team of people who she respected and enjoyed working with every day was the dream job she had prayed for. Jillian was finally soaring.

Soar Like an Eagle

What does it mean for a woman to be duty conscious? The definition of duty is to do something because it is part of your job like the queen's official duty or job. The definition or meaning of conscious is being aware of your surroundings and knowing what is happening in your area. As women, it is our job to be aware of our families and all that happens around them. We are the official caretakers of our family! Like eagles we are to sit high and look low so that we are able to have a larger view of the situations that occur in our Queendom. You do not see eagles walking on the ground because it will change their perspective and they will no longer be the overseer of all situations. It is not that an eagle can't walk on the ground but that is not their duty and it is not their responsibility. If the eagle stays on the ground they will be too close to the situation and will be unable to protect themselves from predators, they will be vulnerable to the environment and to the things they can't see. When an eagle soars they are able to see a larger view of the landscape and see potential problems and concerns before they occur and adjust accordingly based on each situation.

Have you ever studied eagles? Eagles can fly up to 15,000 feet and soar for hours. Eagles do not fly with other birds but fly alone or with other eagles. Their vision is better than humans and they can spot their prey as far as a mile away. The eagle's ability to fly at such great heights and above all other birds provides an advantage to observe the environment.

When an eagle hunts for food such as spotting a fish in a lake or pond it will not panic if it is unable to obtain the fish because the eagle knows there are many other opportunities for another fish because there is more than one pond. The eagle has a global view and will never be concerned with one twig because it is blessed with the entire forest.

Like eagles we are to have a large view of our landscape. As the Queen, we are to "swoop" down and assist in the areas related to our families and communities. We are not to stay in the intimate details but to help facilitate or guide from the side for the enhancement of our family members, and then soar back to our vantage point to manage and assist the family. When eagles soar they use the wind to elevate them and they do not have to work as hard in this process. Isaiah 40: 31 states, "But those who wait upon God get fresh strength. They spread their wings and soar like eagles, they run and don't get tired, they walk and don't lag behind." When women soar we are able to develop a closer relationship with God, and allow God to direct our path in order to hear the direction of what we have been called to do. Like eagles, soaring pushes us to higher heights and allows God to carry us; it is when we soar that God speaks to us, and builds us back up. We are able to rest in his arms to rejuvenate in order to be able to "swoop" back down and assist the family. As a Queen, your job is to be available as situations arise and provide guidance through the problem solving process. When situations are resolved you will fly high again until the next situation requires your time and attention. It is not that you can't sit and solve every small problem, but it is not your role in the Queendom. A woman's job is to take great care of the blessings provided in het territory.

PERSONAL REFLECTION

1. How have you defined your duty to your family in the past? How has it changed in your current situation?

2. How do you take care of your family? How would your family describe your care of them? Overly protective? Tyrant? Helicopter parent? Passive? Uninterested?

3. Do you have a global view of current situations or are you on the ground in the intimate details? If you are on the ground, what changes will you need to make to have a more global view?

4. What is your management style and is it beneficial to your family? How do you communicate and facilitate conversations on a daily or weekly basis?

HELPFUL STUDY

- ❖ Proverbs 14:1, "Lady Wisdom builds a lovely home; Sir Fool comes along and tears it down brick by brick."
- ❖ Isaiah 40:31, "But those who wait upon God get fresh strength. They spread their wings and soar like eagles, they run and don't get tired, they walk and don't lag behind."
- ❖ Revelations 12:14, "The Woman was given wings of a great eagle to fly to a place in the desert to be kept in safety and comfort for a time and times and half a time, safe and sound from the Serpent."
- ❖ 1 Thessalonians 4:11, "Stay calm; mind your own business; do your own job. You've heard all this from us before, but a reminder never hurts. We want you living in a way that will command the respect of outsiders, not lying around sponging off your friends."

Jewel: Not Satisfied With Mediocrity

Proverbs 31:29
"Many women have done wonderful things, but you've outclassed them all!"

Belinda Jones and her sisters were the jewels of their father's eye; everyone knew the Jones sisters. The sisters were exactly 15 months apart and when asked, their father, Maurice, would tell the story of when their mother, Betty, announced she was pregnant with Hazel, the first sister; he bought his wife a beautiful watch to always remember the time he was so happy. When Betty announced she was pregnant with the second daughter, Cynthia, he bought Betty a mink coat to stay warm in his love. When Betty announced she was pregnant with the third daughter, Belinda, he bought her a diamond ring for his love to shine bright. He wanted everyone to know how happy he was to have four beautiful women in his life. Maurice spoiled the girls and always brought something home for each of them. As the girls grew older and started attracting the attention of the opposite sex, Maurice had one rule...no boyfriends or serious dating until the age of 18.

Hazel left home after high school and attended a university four hours from home. Hazel would check on her sisters but between her studies, her job and her new boyfriend she just didn't have time for anything else. Cynthia left home after high school and followed in Hazel's footsteps and attended the same university, but she did not want to work like Hazel and spent most of her time at school parties and hanging out with her friends. Cynthia was smart enough to keep good grades so her parents did not have a reason to bring her home. Belinda did not go to school with her sisters; she decided to stay home and attend the local university. Belinda was able to get an academic scholarship and by staying home she had minimal cost for college.

Hazel married her boyfriend, Ray, who was a nice guy but never completed anything. Ray never completed school, his music career or most jobs. Ray was happy Hazel kept his life together. He did not have to worry about the bills or the house because Hazel took care of everything. Cynthia married John, a guy she used to party with in school and she soon found out that John did not believe in conforming to all of society's rules. John was satisfied living in an apartment for the rest of their lives. He believed that as long as they both worked minimum wage jobs, they could spend their time enjoying life one day at a time. No need to plan for a future with more responsibilities than what they already had.

Belinda loved her sisters, but she wanted to date someone stable like her dad, so she was unwilling to compromise. Belinda finished college with a bachelor's degree in nursing. She did so well that she received another scholarship to become a registered nurse. Her sisters said she was wasting away and her standards were too high, which is why she did not have a boyfriend.

Belinda did not care. She completed school and worked at the local hospital. Belinda was active in her church through the women and nurses ministry and she attended bible study each week. She traveled with the senior ministry when they took local trips and cruises while Hazel and Cynthia always went to their parents for loans or asked them to watch their children so they could go out and party, Belinda was living a financially independent life. The last time Cynthia was home she pulled Belinda aside and said look, "you are going to be 42 next week, what do you have to show for it? A job? Your church? Your standards are too high! No one will ever be like daddy. Do like Hazel and I did and take the next man who asks you out and make it work with him. You will never find a man at the rate you are going." Belinda hugged and kissed her sister and thanked her for the advice but her pastor had just preached a sermon relaying that a woman should never look for a man because a man will find his good thing. Belinda was happy and content because she had a great job, a wonderful church family and her parents were healthy and happy.

A year later a new doctor, Dr. Nelson, joined the hospital staff. He attended and later joined Belinda's church. Nelson would sit next to Belinda in bible study and soon became her prayer partner. One day after church, Nelson asked Belinda if he could take her to the movies and dinner. Belinda accepted and they dated for a year when Nelson finally asked Belinda to marry him. Belinda married Nelson at the young age of 45 and Nelson told her every day she was his good thing.

Unknown Territory

Have you ever settled for something less than what you wanted or what you deserved? Have you ever believed what was promised to you would never arrive? Proverbs 3:5-6, "Trust God from the bottom of your heart; don't try to figure out everything on your own. Listen for God's voice in everything you do, everywhere you go; He's the one who will keep you on track". This scripture is telling you to trust only in God because He will secure your path. Not only must you trust in God but you must wait for God to act on His time. While you are in your waiting season, God is growing and preparing you for the next level. God wants you to enjoy the dull, ordinary, routine places of your life which He has given you so that He knows you can handle the next level. If you listen to the voices of your family, friends and co-workers over God's voice then your walk and path may not be smooth.

When we listen and obey then our walk and experience is much more enjoyable.

My daughter has played volleyball since she was in the sixth grade for her schools and Amateur Athletic Union teams. Her dream during high school was to be recruited to play volleyball at a Division 1 university. Every waking moment during high school was practice, travel to volleyball tournaments and volleyball games. She has traveled throughout the United States playing at different volleyball tournaments. During her senior year she was recruited to several Division 2 and Division 3 universities and we spent time visiting the schools, looking at their academic programs and viewing her options. As graduation grew close my mother voice took over as I pushed her to, "take the bird in your hand and stop waiting for the bird in the bush". My number one university option was not my daughter's. It was actually last on her list. It happened to be the university her brother attended. The school offered her the most money to play volleyball and as we sat in orientation, it was clear she was not happy with this choice but she was going to commit anyway. She had not signed her official paperwork for the school, but after orientation my husband and I knew this was her destiny, or so we thought. On July 17 my daughter had a conversation with a coach at a Division 1 school. He was interested in her after viewing her volleyball video tape. We traveled 14 hours to meet the coach, view the school and check out if this could be a possibility for her. In the end, not only was it a possibility, but the coach needed her back at the university in five days for orientation and practice. We shifted everything, scheduled doctor appointments, transferred records and traveled another 14 hours back home, to turn right back around and drive another 14 hours in order to bring her back to the university by Monday.

My husband and I flew to New Orleans to watch her play her first collegiate volleyball game three weeks later. I was extremely proud to watch her play, but I was even prouder that she had enough sense to continue to pray and not settle for less than her dream, even with her mother in her ear. I wanted her at the school with her brother because she has some medical challenges and I knew he would help her if she became ill. It would have been easier to get to her if she were only three hours away from home versus 14 hours, so quite naturally I based my decision on convenience. I am proud she did not stop praying and she waited for God's word and plan. She has done extremely well academically and medically. And while she has had a few health challenges, God has placed amazing people in her life at the university and in the community. Her brother said his prayers were answered too, because he didn't want her to attend "his" school and be in his business.

The enemy is good about planting seeds to kill a dream; this is the best you can do, you will never have what you want or other people are more qualified than you. Kick those thoughts out of your mind and do not settle for mediocrity! If you have ever played cards you know that sometimes you get a great hand and sometimes you are dealt a bad hand. Learn how to play a bad hand well and find joy in just being in the game until your next hand is dealt. Settle in God's promise and know that His will be done. Have patience and know that He is growing you during your time of wait and preparing you for your blessings.

PERSONAL REFLECTION

1. Have you settled for something less than what God has called in your life? Did you know you settled and what was your reasoning?

2. Do you struggle with waiting for your blessing or new season? What is your fear?

3. Describe a time when your prayers were answered and reflect on the lessons you learned prior to the answer.

4. When negative thoughts enter your mind what can you do to combat these thoughts?

HELPFUL STUDY

- ❖ Romans 12:1-2, "So here's what I want you to do, God helping you: Take your everyday, ordinary life—your sleeping, eating, going-to-work, and walking-around life—and place it before God as an offering. Embracing what God does for you is the best thing you can do for him. Don't become so well-adjusted to your culture that you fit into it without even thinking. Instead, fix your attention on God. You'll be changed from the inside out. Readily recognize what he wants from you, and quickly respond to it. Unlike the culture around you, always dragging you down to its level of immaturity, God brings the best out of you, develops well-formed maturity in you."

- ❖ Colossians 3:15-17, "Let the peace of Christ keep you in tune with each other, in step with each other. None of this going off and doing your own thing. And cultivate thankfulness. Let the Word of Christ—the Message—have the run of the house. Give it plenty of room in your lives. Instruct and direct one another using good common sense. And sing, sing your hearts out to God! Let every detail in your lives—words, actions, whatever—be done in the name of the Master, Jesus, thanking God the Father every step of the way."

- Philippians 4:13, "Whatever I have, wherever I am, I can make it through anything in the One who makes me who I am."

Conclusion

Jewel: A Woman Of God Who Is Worthy To Be Praised

A woman of God who is worthy to be praised is YOU! I hope the jewels found in this book will help you grow in your Queendom. Each jewel is important and will help remind you of the significant role we have as women. We are unique and wonderfully made!

I was facilitating a session at a Women's Conference and their theme was "Reflections of a Lovely Lady" using Proverbs 31:30, *"Charm can mislead and beauty soon fades. The woman to be admired and praised is the woman who lives in the Reverence-of-God."* As I prepared for the conference I was filled with such joy and clarity around the characteristics of the Virtuous Woman that I wanted every woman to possess the jewels of this Lovely Lady. Statistics show the current divorce rate of married couples lingers around 40 percent to 50 percent which has increased over the last 20 years. Based on this data, I understand why after the conference, women asked me for my notes. Several women shared they wished they had this information before they married and some wanted the jewels for their everyday living. As I have shared throughout this book, I am fortunate and honored to have been married to Patrick for 25 years. We work at our marriage constantly and through the work we have a loving and satisfying marriage. I look forward to waking up next to him every day. It was when another woman approached me and said she too had been married to her husband for over 30 years but she was not happy and wanted more information about the jewels. I was very clear with the conference participants that some of the jewels are easy and some require hard work. We are all unique, therefore how we approach each jewel will also be unique. The jewels provide us the opportunity to model and practice Christ-like behavior every day! The best part of the conversation is knowing we have a Father who knows our every need and gives us everything we need to be successful. He will grow us in ways we can't comprehend.

My prayer is you will use the jewels as your personal "Guide to Queendom Living". All Hail the Queen!

Reference Page

1. Peterson, Eugene H. The Message (MSG). Bible Gateway. Web. Copyright 1993, 1994, 1995, 1996, 2000, 2001, and 2002.

2. Thomas, Peggy and Park, Edwards. Odd Tales from the Smithsonian. Smithsonian Institution Press, 1986.

CPSIA information can be obtained
at www.ICGtesting.com
Printed in the USA
BVOW08*1958141216
470700BV00005B/75/P